Religion and the Politics of Tolerance

Religion and the Politics of Tolerance

How Christianity Builds Democracy

Marie A. Eisenstein

BAYLOR UNIVERSITY PRESS

Cover Designer: Stephanie Blumenthal
Cover Image: Cartoon# 0076063 from The Granger Collection.
Used by Permission

Library of Congress Cataloging-in-Publication Data

Eisenstein, Marie Ann.
Religion and the politics of tolerance : how Christianity builds democracy / Marie Ann Eisenstein.
p. cm.
Includes bibliographical references and index.
ISBN 978-1-932792-84-3 (alk. paper)
1. Religion and politics--United States. 2. Democracy--Religious aspects. 3. Toleration--Religious aspects. I. Title.

BL2525.E418 2008
261.7--dc22

2007026447

Printed in the United States of America on acid-free paper with a minimum of 30% pcw recycled content.

To the G-d of all creation,
the G-d who encompasses all and is all and
who is the author and creator of everything.

Table of Contents

List of Tables and Figures

TABLES

Figures

Acknowledgments

In producing this book, I owe a debt of gratitude to many individuals who encouraged, guided, and helped me through this process. I know I cannot list them all. My husband Maurice Eisenstein and my parents Ronald and Rose Prescaro have been consistent sources of encouragement, strength, and support. Where or who would I be without you?

To Carey Newman at Baylor University Press; thank you for believing in my manuscript. You are the publisher of my first book and for that I am truly grateful. I hope that it is the first (but not the best) among many more to come.

To Ted Jelen and Laura Olson, both of whom willingly and speedily reviewed everything I asked them to review for me. I truly appreciate your gifts of time, effort, and intellect.

To Indiana University Northwest for granting me summer fellowships during 2005 and 2006 that enabled me to work on and complete this manuscript. Thank you.

Introduction

Certainly, no power to prescribe any religious exercise, or to assume authority in religious discipline, has been delegated to the General Government. It must then rest with the States, as far as it can be in any human authority.

—Thomas Jefferson to Samuel Miller, January 23, 1808

The American political landscape is replete with the perceived incompatibility between our political ideals and religious beliefs. In the U.S. Constitution, the First Amendment exemplifies this very contradiction even within its religious clauses. Of all the rights enumerated in the Bill of Rights, only religion has spelled-out dual and frequently contradictory rights—the establishment clause and the free exercise clause. The state cannot favor any particular religion over any other; and as it is frequently interpreted in contemporary jurisprudence, it cannot favor any religion at all. Simultaneously, the state cannot act in any way to prevent an individual's exercise of his or her religious belief. The first clause requires the state to be neutral in all religious matters—in a sense, putting the state above religion. The second clause requires the state to recognize the supremacy of religious practices over the everyday concerns of the state. Recently, France passed a law banning all exterior expressions of religious beliefs in public schools, deeming this necessary for upholding the secular nature of the French political state. In the United States, this fulfills the first clause (the establishment clause), but is antithetical to the second clause (the free exercise clause). Americans would recognize that secularization is a positive act and abridges an inherent right.

The Jeffersonian Influence

Perhaps no other single individual has had more influence on our modern interpretation of the First Amendment religious clauses and on our twenty-first-century notions of appropriate church-state relations than Thomas Jefferson. Actually, it was James Madison who penned the religious clauses of the First Amendment while Jefferson was in France—and Madison was as much a supporter of religious freedom as Jefferson. It is also recognized that Madison's written defense of the religious clauses is as important to the founding of this country as Jefferson's. Nonetheless, in contemporary political discussion concerning the constitutional interpretation of the political role of religion, Jefferson consistently prevails as the preeminent voice. "Jefferson's architectural metaphor, in the course of time, has achieved virtual canonical status and become more familiar to the American people than the actual text of the First Amendment" (Dreisbach 2002, 3).

In 1802, as president of the United States, Thomas Jefferson penned a letter to the Danbury Baptist Association of Connecticut. In it, he stated:

> Believing with you that religion is a matter which lies solely between Man & His God, that he owes account to none other for his faith or his worship, that the legitimate powers of government reach actions only, & not opinions, I contemplate with sovereign reverence that act of the whole American people which declared that their legislature should "make no law respecting an establishment of religion, or prohibiting the free exercise thereof," thus building *a wall of separation between Church & State* (Dreisbach 2002, 1–2; italics added).

From his bully pulpit as the third president of the United States, Jefferson took up the issue of religious freedom when he was compelled to espouse his views of the religious clauses in the First Amendment, Jefferson wrote the letter to the Danbury Baptists to address the stiff political criticism he was receiving from the federalists, and it provided him a public venue to identify his "wall" analogy. As an ardent anti-federalist with a profound commitment to dual federalism, Jefferson refused to declare national days of fasting or thanksgiving, believing that such declarations were beyond the purview of the national government. Such declarations were appropriate for the individual state authority, but not for national or federal authority. However, Jefferson's refusal to pronounce days of fasting and thanksgiving reflects both his commitment to ensuring appropriate church-state relations and his views concerning federalism's boundaries between state and national authority. Jefferson, with the phrase "a wall of separation" indicated unequivocally his reading and understanding of the religious clauses of the First Amendment.

Jefferson's statement in the Danbury letter is consistent with his long-held, lifelong views concerning church-state relations. Although his statements on freedom of the press may be less than perfectly consistent over time, the same cannot be said for church and state. Leonard Levy, surely the harshest critic of Jefferson's overall record in civil rights and liberties, conceded but one area in which he felt adulation was well deserved—the relationship between government and religion. Only one other president ever refused to issue thanksgiving proclamations because he felt such a decree would cross the line between church and state. In countless other ways, the Jeffersonian commitment to separation is remarkably clear and consistent, despite the political hazards of an arguably godless philosophy (O'Neil 1999, 793).

An example of one of the "countless other ways" in which Jefferson demonstrated his commitment to separation between church and state is in his support of free and tax-supported nonsectarian public schools (Wood 1979). In short, Jefferson's Danbury letter clearly articulated both his commitment to and philosophy of inflexible separation between church and state as an appropriate relationship. Though none of us in twenty-first-century America can escape the imprint of the "wall of separation" metaphor upon our national psyche, the phrase was a mere historical anecdote until it surfaced in 1879. After that, it remained dormant until 1947. From that point on, however, the "wall of separation" has grown to become part and parcel of our national identity in discussions regarding the religious clauses in the First Amendment.

With the 1879 *Reynolds v. United States* case, the Supreme Court for the first time employed the "wall of separation" metaphor in one of its decisions. Reynolds, a case about the free exercise of religion as opposed to the establishment clause, stands as one of the few cases dealing with either of the religious clauses of the First Amendment during the first 150 years of American history. In a thorough and engaging scholarly assessment as to why the Supreme Court in 1879 used this phrase in one of its decisions, the answer turns on the ironic (Dreisbach 2002, chap. 7). The 1879 Court sought to delineate that while the national legislature could proscribe behavior, it could not proscribe opinion (regarding religion). In the 1802 Danbury letter, Jefferson stated that "the legitimate powers of government reach actions only, & not opinion" (Dreisbach 2002, 48). However, the word "legitimate" had been incorrectly transcribed as "legislative" and, as a result, Jefferson's Danbury letter served the very purpose of the 1879 Court when it sought to support the Court's ruling that religious action deemed contrary to the public good can be legislated against while opinion cannot be subject to the actions of the legislature.

Thomas Jefferson's "wall of separation" was now a part of constitutional jurisprudence and the metaphor was now part of the American lexicon. It would remain dormant and not become common parlance, as we now recognize the reference, until 1947. In the words of Kenneth D. Wald (2003, 90), "In 1947 the Court decided a case that was to herald a flood of litigation about the modern meaning of First Amendment prohibitions 'respecting an establishment of religion.'" The case was *Everson v. Board of Education*. In that case, Justice Black, writing for the majority, concluded that "(t)he First Amendment has erected a wall of separation between church and state. That wall must be kept high and impregnable. We could not approve the slightest breach" (Alley 1999, 54). Nonetheless, the majority opinion in the Everson case upheld New Jersey's funding of bus transportation for parochial school students, which many individuals today would find counter-intuitive to the above statement made by Justice Black. "Although the outcome in *Everson v. Board of Education* was beneficial to the religious students who were the recipients of public transportation, the majority's analysis was decidedly unfavorable to their long-term First Amendment position" (Reid 2003, 82). The opinion in Everson was that New Jersey had not breached the wall of separation between church and state, but, in the future, such breaches would be accepted only under the narrowest of circumstances.

With the Everson case, the "wall of separation" rose from an obscure background reference to the front and center of American constitutional jurisprudence regarding the First Amendment religious clauses. The phrase was no longer to be solely a metaphor; it would become "a virtual rule of constitutional law" (Dreisbach 2002, 3). The Everson case marks our modern understanding and interpretation of the religious clauses, particularly as it pertains to what constitutes an establishment of religion. After Everson, many cases regarding the religious clauses of the First Amendment came before the Supreme Court; however, issues regarding the public school system were most important both in terms of number of cases and the substance of Court decisions. Writing in 1979 about the place of religion within the context of public education, James E. Wood Jr. stated: "During the past thirty years no other church-state issues have provoked as much litigation" (1979, 64). The same can still be said today. More importantly, the Everson case made clear that the historical writings of Jefferson (and Madison as well) were the basis for determining just what the religious clauses in the First Amendment were intended to mean.

Soon thereafter, in 1948, the next important case to establish the wall of separation as the "virtual rule" of constitutional law for the establishment clause was *McCollum v. Board of Education.* Using the logic articulated in Everson, in which a breach of the wall of separation between church and state could be allowed in only the narrowest circumstances and that the wall must be "high and impregnable," the Court found in the McCollum case that the wall had been breached. The McCollum case asserted that allowing religious instruction to take place during regular school hours—even if the students did so voluntarily—constituted an establishment of religion. With Everson and McCollum, "an imposing edifice has been constructed" (Reid 2003, 87) and "the Supreme Court expanded its use of the prohibition of establishments in the early 1960s to school prayer" (2003, 87).

Engel v. Vitale in 1962 was the first significant case on the question of school prayer. The case dealt with the New York Regents' Prayer "a nondenominational invocation to be recited daily by teachers in the public school system. School children were free to choose whether or not to participate. In yet another opinion by Hugo Black, the Court struck down the practice" (Reid 2003, 87). The next important case on the matter of school prayer was *Abington School District v. Schempp.* In Abington, the Supreme Court again ruled against the school district for requiring the reading of Bible verses and saying the Lord's Prayer at the beginning of each school day. The Court's rulings in both Engel and Abington strongly endorsed the concept that any religious conduct promoted or facilitated by an institution of government (such as a public school paid for by tax dollars) represents an establishment of religion and constitutes a breach of that wall of separation advocated by Jefferson (Wald 2003, 91). Jefferson's phrase had now become the accepted and recognized basis for interpreting the establishment clause in the First Amendment.

Theory versus Practice

Thomas Jefferson defined the relationship between American politics and religion as one of absolute separation between church and state. Not only did he famously call for a high "wall" between the two, but the Supreme Court repeatedly has applied his "wall of separation" in its interpretation of church-state relations. The fact is, however, that the practice of separation has not proved to be true in fact or in predominant citizen belief. Rather, the "absolute" separation of religion and state has remained fluid and changeable over time—the result of two conflicting clauses on religious practice in the Constitution. In a liberal democracy, one can pursue an absolute separation of church and state, but one cannot ask for or pursue an absolute separation of religion and politics. These are two radically different pursuits; the first one is institutional, the latter is behavioral. The relationship between religion and politics is at the individual level because it is there that political will is exercised; therefore, it is counter-intuitive to believe that a religious individual can, in any meaningful way, divorce himself or herself from a professed set of beliefs when behaving as a political actor. This is what the free exercise clause is intended to protect. Partly because of the inherent tension between the separation of institutions and the free exercise of individuals, the Court found that unequivocal application of Jefferson's separationist interpretation "proved surprisingly difficult" (Schotten & Stevens 1996, 69).[1]

The important issues to address are the reasons that Thomas Jefferson felt the need for a comprehensive and absolute separation between church and state and the reasons that the American political system, uniquely, found it necessary to protect not solely religion from the state but, significantly, the state from religion. Thomas Jefferson's enlightenment perspective accepted the inherent incompatibility of religious belief and liberal democratic politics—a perspective that rests on the idea that the very action of expressing religious belief requires an individual to be intolerant of other individuals of dissimilar beliefs. This enlightenment perception was that religion is about absolutes and liberal democratic politics is about compromise and tolerance (i.e., being a gracious loser); therefore, it is impossible to practice both within the same arena. In John Dewey's terms, liberal democratic politics was for the public arena and religion was for the private arena.

The dichotomy that politics is for the public arena and religion for the private arena has not only defined American perception of the First Amendment, but it also has made modern political science a component of modern democratic theory. Intolerance is the major threat to both the establishment of liberal democracy and the continued functioning of established liberal democracies. Intolerance, which rejects the legitimacy of other individuals to equally participate in the political process, preordains who does and does not have legitimacy before the political process. This preordination, therefore, negates the need to compromise. Intolerance is not limited solely to religious individuals, but religious individuals often are perceived to be consistently the most intolerant. The greater the level of religious commitment, the less tolerance one has for others of dissimilar beliefs. Therefore, the individual of high religious commitment is less likely to promote liberal democracy and its requirement of tolerance—especially when he or she is in power.

The theoretical logic of the arguments that have held sway against religion and the democratic value of tolerance (or its negative intolerance) since the writing of the U.S. Constitution is consistent with the enlightenment perspective on religiosity, and it can be understood in terms of classical liberal opposition to the church. But it is not clear that this attribute of religion is an accurate representation, especially within modern American liberal democratic practice. Alternatively, it can be argued that the very nature of religion has gone through a metamorphosis in the United States, making religious individuals no less tolerant, or possibly more tolerant, than their less religious neighbors. It is possible that the socialization of American liberal democratic values that permeate religion in the United States negates the European tradition of intolerance for which religion has been ascribed by the Jeffersonian enlightenment. These are the central themes of this book.

Religious Faith and Tolerance

The historical expressions of intolerance by identifiably religious individuals are well known. What is frequently overlooked and therefore not attributed to religious faith is its responsibility for major acts of tolerance in American history. Abolition was a movement supported not only by the dominant forms of Christianity of the time but had its roots in the Quaker opposition to slavery in the late seventeenth century (Butler, Wacker, & Balmer 2003, 202). Another is the Civil Rights movement that had large Catholic and Jewish religious initiation and support, along with the leadership of Reverend Martin Luther King Jr., who used overtly religious language and themes. Then there is social welfare, which is best exemplified by the Catholic Church as it established hospitals and other institutions in many parts of America to provide for those in need.

It is less known that the modern evangelical movement, in large part, was started in California by a black preacher and former hotel waiter named William J. Seymour. This new Pentecostal movement was known as the Azusa Street Revival and drew national and international recognition, to a great extent, because of its tolerance of whites and blacks worshiping together. Not only was the Azusa Street Pentecostal movement racially integrated (as were others across the nation), but also women preachers had equal participation. This tolerant religion spread across the country, in the north and south, and its own national newspaper developed. All this occurred in 1905 (Butler et al. 2003, 335–36). This tradition of gender and racial tolerance has continued today in many of the evangelical churches where racial integration is the norm and women preachers have full equality.

We owe to these individuals the enhancement of our understanding of religions' role in the United States in its relationship to the nature of political tolerance in particular and liberal democracy in general. The central argument of this book is straightforward: religion is not the dominant threat to liberal democracy in the United States that it is so often portrayed to be. Alan Wolfe states:

> Religious believers blend into the modern American landscape. They increasingly live in suburbs, send their children to four-year liberal-arts colleges, work in professional capacities, enjoy contemporary music, shop in malls, raise confused and uncertain

> children, and relate primarily to other people with whom they share common interests (Wolfe 2003, 255).

Wolfe makes the case that religion in America has gone through dramatic changes including "a palpable increase in religious toleration that extends to non-Christians" (Wolfe 2003, 248). Yet, as Wolfe indicates, these dramatic changes have been hardly noticed in the public arena, particularly by intellectuals who act as though "Jonathan Edwards is still preaching and his congregation is still quaking in fear" (Wolfe 2003, 249). Thus, the argument of this book may be a simple statement, but demonstrating the argument, which is the task at hand, is complex and full of challenges.

Scope of Project

The central themes of this book—liberal democracy, political tolerance, and religion—are weighty themes. Likewise, supporting the foundational argument of this book—that religion is not a dominant threat to liberal democracy in the United States, particularly as it relates to political tolerance—is a weighty undertaking. These themes are continuously discussed, debated, and analyzed in various academic fields including, but not limited to, political theory, philosophy, history, religious studies, comparative studies in political science and religion, the psychology of religion, and sociology (in particular, the sociology of religion), in addition to scholarship that tackles these issues from the perspective of legal tradition.[2] Furthermore, within each of these various academic postures, the methodological norms of what constitutes scholarly investigation and analysis differs (statistical, experimental, ethnographic, hagiographic, hermeneutic, case study, etc.), which means within two different academic perspectives analogous discussions may be occurring but the scholarly literature for each venue is separate and unique. In short, there are other approaches to studying the topic and issues of religion and political tolerance than that which is presented here.

This book, though, is not intended to be considered interdisciplinary or cross-disciplinary in nature. It does not pretend or claim to incorporate the comprehensive intellectual grasp of all the various academic disciplines in which issues of liberal democracy, religion, and political tolerance are discussed, debated, and analyzed. Also, this work does not touch upon, let alone encompass, the breadth, width, and depth of these various academic arenas. As an empirically trained political scientist, I approach this topic from a perspective that is very much influenced by empirical social science in methodology and issue framing. Therefore, this book is most appropriately placed within the academic discipline of political science in general, and the religion and politics subfield, in particular. Consequently, the literature I use to inform the discussion and analyses throughout this book is drawn predominantly from works familiar to academicians within political science. Specifically, the literature regarding political tolerance is from within mainstream political science scholarship while the literature regarding religion/religiosity primarily is from the religion and politics subfield of political science.[3] In this book, I reference some works that fall outside of what I call the academic "silo" of political science. But this is only to admit, right from the start, that for those whose expertise falls outside of the predominantly quantitative field of political science, this book will not do justice to the considerable scholarship committed to these topics, especially when their expertise falls outside the particular area of inquiry represented in this work.

In chapter 1, I review the concept of political tolerance, which places the text explicitly within the mainstream political science scholarship as well as the religion and politics literature. Bringing together these two literary arenas provides the basis and rationale for the whole book, which includes chapters that reexamine the relationship between religion and political tolerance in liberal democracy and that support the contention that religion is not the threat to liberal democracy that it generally has been purported to be. Beginning with chapter 2, I bring a multiplicity of data sources to bear on this topic, including an examination of data from a random sample phone survey of 600 respondents (a purely quantitative undertaking). I marshal empirical evidence from structural equation modeling to begin to make the case for a new understanding of the link between religion/religiosity and political tolerance.

In chapter 3, I utilize focus group research (a qualitative technique not common to political science scholarship). It is important to hear, in their own words, what individuals of faith have to say about the relationship between faith and democracy. Therefore, I turn to a qualitative assessment of the linkage between modern Christian congregants and their understanding of the relationship between their faith and their role as citizens in a liberal democracy. The primary purpose of this chapter is to explore how religious individuals navigate the relationship between their faith and participation in a liberal democracy, which, in general, includes political tolerance.

In chapter 4, I analyze data from a survey-based experimental design and begin to address the potential linkages between issue-attitude positions and political tolerance. Because of the intense current debate over social and moral issues, this chapter addresses that debate and is essential for no other reason than the popular perception, as it relates to what colloquially can be called "conservative Christian right" attitudes toward various topics (such as abortion and homosexual marriage) are often considered *a priori* proof of political intolerance. Given the importance in today's politically charged environment between hot-button political issue attitudes and perceptions of tolerance versus intolerance, empirical research examining potential linkages is a necessary and important area of scholarship.

Chapter 5 concludes with a summary of the overall findings of the book and brings together all the various research strands to paint a contemporary picture of religion and religiosity in America as it relates to political tolerance. In this final chapter, all the information from the previous chapters come together as I argue for a positive—not negative—relationship between religion and religiosity and liberal democracy in the United States.

Before we move into chapter 1, two additional caveats need to be expressed. First, throughout this book—chapters 2, 3, and 4 in particular—my goal is to address, with a multiplicity of methods (including quantitative, qualitative, and experimental), the relationship between religion, political tolerance, and liberal democracy. However, all three data sets used in this book are drawn from a single place—Lake County, Indiana. This means that although the discussion of religion, political tolerance, and liberal democracy is one of national import, the particular data used in that discussion is regional in nature. The specific limitations and unique regional attributes of each data set are discussed, as needed, in the chapters in which each data set is employed.

I do not want to understate the applicability of my findings based upon my data sets. There is valid reason to conclude that similarity in religiosity and political tolerance in one Midwestern county can be expected to exist in other Midwestern counties. The data here are from a single county within a single state, and questions undoubtedly will follow regarding how we can generalize from this data. But there is, I believe, a legitimate argument to be made that these samples are representative of the beliefs and attitudes of "middle America." In the same way, I do not want to overstate the applicability of my findings. The data sets are generally smaller than ideally desired, which has its drawbacks and raises questions about the ability to generalize. But the data sets are adequate to allow the findings presented here to be considered highly suggestive, even though they ultimately cannot be deemed conclusive.

Finally, this book deals strictly with religion within the context of a modern American political system. There is no argument that the models proposed in this book would be universally applicable outside their political context, such as laterally to Muslims in Saudi Arabia or retrospectively to more theocratic societies. For example, because of their religious history, Catholics in Mexico will have different political values than Catholics in the United States. The analyses throughout this book rely upon a concept of political tolerance consistent with a liberal democratic society. Furthermore, these analyses rely on a unique integration of the values of liberal democracy with the experience of religion and religiosity within America in the twenty-first century.

Chapter 1
The Politics of Tolerance

> America has from the beginning been a nation bent on redemption. That, after all, is what John Winthrop was getting at in 1630 when he famously predicted, "We shall be a city upon a hill." The struggle to define what needs saving by whom has been fought out continually on a variety of battlefields. And it continues today, in what Nobel laureate Robert Foel recently called our "Fourth Great Awakening": a new religious revival fueled by revulsion with the corruptions of a contemporary society.
>
> —*Michael Kazin, "The Politics of Devotion" in* The Nation, *April 6, 1998*

The more things change the more they remain the same. In every generation, religion invades the public square, or so it might appear to a casual observer. With that "invasion" comes the concomitant reification of political tolerance. Although political tolerance is an important virtue, particularly in a liberal democracy, it is not the only virtue; but when the issue is religion, political tolerance is the only virtue that can command center stage. Nevertheless, political tolerance is also a virtue that religious individuals in the United States routinely have been accused of lacking. Religious individuals are perceived in this way, in part, because clear distinctions between the public and private spheres of behavior no longer exist. What was once private behavior, encompassing objectionable values, is part of and central to the public sphere. As such, it now becomes incumbent upon all citizens to accept and support (or reject) the new public values, especially in terms of legal equality (Eisenstein 2005).

The resulting incompatibility of orthodox religious values with liberal democracy's acceptance of varied personal lifestyles is exacerbated by the contradiction between the demands for religious expression to remain in its private sphere and the simultaneous pressure of secularism to be accepted as appropriate democratic expression in the public arena. The crux of the problem is that a secular view of alternative lifestyles is accepted in the public square, while the religious view is rejected there and deemed acceptable solely in the private sphere. Thus, no issue of tolerance exists with those who advocate for homosexual marriage, but an inherent intolerance does exist for those who disagree with homosexual marriage because of religious values. However, the maintenance of the conflict between the public and private sphere is unnecessary. The freedoms prized in a liberal democracy do not require acceptance of another's values or perspectives; it requires tolerance (Eisenstein 2005). Understanding what tolerance is and what tolerance is not is central to any meaningful assessment of how religion and political tolerance intersect. Given the centrality of political tolerance, its meaning and application, the first task is to give a definition to this important concept.

Defining Tolerance

Political tolerance is a difficult concept. It has what Sullivan, Piereson & Marcus (1982) call a confusing relationship to other concepts such as (absence of) prejudice, notions of democracy, religious toleration, and open-mindedness. When political tolerance is connected to or used interchangeably with these other concepts, clarity finds a way of escaping and the waters in which tolerance resides get murky. Nevertheless, accurately defining and ultimately measuring tolerance is necessary before any analysis can be undertaken.

In everyday conversation, for the most part, tolerance is used whenever someone disagrees with another, particularly when the position is well known and accepted within popular circles. Abortion is an excellent example. The popular and accepted orthodoxy is that abortion is and should be an individual (the woman's) choice. Any position contrary to this is intolerant. The problem with this use and definition of tolerance is that it is entirely inaccurate. Political tolerance, as used and defined within empirical political science scholarship, has a very particular meaning and has nothing to do with whether or not an individual agrees with any particular set of issue positions. Political tolerance is not about attitudes; it is not synonymous with a set of particular attitudes on a set of particular topics wherein if you do not fall into agreement with the norms of the day, then you are intolerant. Political tolerance is about actions, not attitudes. For an excellent discussion of this distinction, see Andrew Murphy's 1997 article "Tolerance, Toleration, and the Liberal Tradition." While Murphy's suggested terms are not used to differentiate between actions and attitudes, his argument that a distinction does and must exist between these two in order for a proper understanding of political tolerance to exist is incorporated into how political tolerance is used and measured.

Political tolerance as a concept "implies a willingness to 'put up with' those things one rejects or opposes. Politically, it implies a willingness to permit the expression of ideas or interests one opposes" (Sullivan et al. 1982, 2). When depicted in this manner, political tolerance is broadly construed. "In a narrower sense, tolerance is closely associated with the idea of procedural fairness" (Sullivan et al. 1982, 2). Focusing on procedure rather than on substance means that as long as one is willing to apply the "rules of the game" equally, then that individual is tolerant. As with Sullivan et al., the authors Nunn, Crockett, and Williams (1978, 12) state, "Tolerance is a straightforward attitude that allows people to have freedom of expression even though one may feel that their ideas are incorrect or even immoral." Marcus et al. (1995, 3) states, "[p]olitical tolerance requires that democratic citizens and leaders secure the full political rights of expression and political participation of groups they find objectionable." In short, political tolerance is the action of allowing those with whom you disagree to practice their constitutionally asserted civil liberties. Political tolerance is when you allow those with whom you disagree the freedom to practice their constitutional rights in the promotion of their own views.

According to Nunn, Crockett, and Williams (1978, 12), one of the biggest misconceptions regarding tolerance involves equating tolerance with acceptance. "Acceptance is to agree with or condone the opinions, values, and behavior of others who are perhaps initially different from oneself." Acceptance is something quite different from tolerance. Thus, the word "oppose" is essential in conceptualizing tolerance. It makes no sense to speak of an individual being tolerant of ideas or groups with whom he or she agrees. If the person is indifferent, he or she cannot be tolerant. Indifference to an idea or group is simply not the same as opposition to an idea or group.

Defining tolerance in a manner in which opposition is central to its conceptualization (and operationalization) is preferable to other definitions. Gibson and Bingham (1985, 604) define political tolerance as "a willingness to extend the rights of citizenship to all members of the polity—that is, to allow political freedoms to those who are politically different." However, Gibson and Bingham's definition leaves the potential to define as tolerance the willingness to extend civil liberties to a "politically different" group with whom one may find oneself in agreement. Using a definition for political tolerance that may or may not include the act of forbearance or endurance does not adequately capture the act of political tolerance.

In earlier research, the frequent definition of tolerance was acceptance of abstract norms of democratic procedure (McCloskey 1964, 361–82). However, defining tolerance as acceptance of abstract norms of democracy leads to a substantial gap between theory and practice. Theoretically, 90 percent of Americans overwhelmingly agree that they believe in free speech for all, regardless of others' views (McCloskey & Brill 1983, 50). But when individuals are asked a more substantive and less abstract question that requires a concrete application of a general principle, such as willingness to extend free speech to a disliked group, individual willingness to extend this particular civil liberty drops below 50 percent. As the work of McCloskey and Brill (1983) demonstrates, relying upon questions in the abstract regarding support for democratic norms versus asking about a concrete application of a general principle leads to an overestimation of political tolerance. Moreover, support for democratic norms in the abstract or acceptance of abstract norms of democracy, has proved more useful as a predictor of political tolerance than as a definition of it (Sullivan et al. 1982; Marcus et al. 1995).

At this point, it is important to clarify concepts of positive and negative liberty, as conceptualized by the British political philosopher Isaiah Berlin, and not to confuse them with notions of positive and negative political tolerance. For example, the Amish have a right to be left alone. Based on Berlin's conceptualization of liberty, we would identify that as the "negative" liberty to be left alone from state interference (in contrast to positive liberties such as freedom to be educated or freedom to be employed). However, willingness to be left alone to structure your own existence or community, presumably in nonpolitical ways (as demonstrated by the Amish), is not an example of the Amish practicing political tolerance. In exercising the negative liberty of "freedom from" state interference to structure their individual lives as they deem appropriate, the Amish are not being required to endure the opinions, practices, or beliefs of individuals or groups that they find objectionable (even vehemently so), which would be a breach of their negative liberty.

Brief Historical Exegesis: Toleration to Tolerance

The concept of political tolerance as discussed and measured in this book is the product of a long history on the theory and philosophy behind the very conceptualization of "toleration," particularly as it relates to the social life of religious practices. Any discussion of the concept of toleration can go as far back as Socrates' dialogical method as a means of searching for "truth" (Stetson & Conti 2005, 26–28). However, toleration did not become a topic of serious philosophical import or concern until sixteenth- and seventeenth-century Europe—when it was centered largely on religious toleration (Sullivan et al. 1982, 3). During that time, several important philosophers wrote on the topic, including Baruch Spinoza and John Locke.

In his poignant "A Letter Concerning Toleration," Locke focused on the relationship between what he called the "State," meaning an official political or governmental authority, and individual religious belief. Locke's writings on tolerance have been universally influential on the Western idea of political tolerance. When applying tolerance to religion, Locke argued that the political authority (or governmental authority, in the case of the United States) should not interfere with an individual's religious beliefs. To Locke, these were two distinct spheres of knowledge and action. Religious belief was between the individual and his or her God and therefore was private. By definition, political action, on the other hand, had consequences for all. For Locke, the only way to enforce religious homogeneity would be through violence or use of force upon the individual, which would negate the justification for government and replace legitimate government with illegitimate government (tyranny). Legitimate government was still governed by natural law and therefore could still act to prohibit individual action of sin or actions that would undermine the social or economic order. These distinctions by Locke become what we today recognize as the legitimate distinction or separation between civil authority and religious authority. Civil authority is concerned with peace and security of the whole, whereas religious authority is concerned with the individual and his or her relationship with the divine. This was also reflected in Locke's argument concerning knowledge. Although Locke is recognized as an empiricist, he was a traditional Christian in his belief. He distinguished between knowledge attained through the senses and reason and knowledge attained through revelation. Government ought, then, to concern itself with things of this world (with sense and reason) and not with religious beliefs that deal inherently with another realm in which knowledge is attained through revealed Scripture. In many ways, Locke's writings inform the ideological founding of the United States, beginning with the Declaration of Independence (including social contract theory and inalienable rights), as well as the Constitution, which defined a secular government by endorsing no nationally recognized religious adherence. Although the idea of political toleration began as a concept that applied predominantly to religious toleration, it has been expanded to other types of toleration, specifically in liberal democracies, toward beliefs and opinions in general and political beliefs in particular.

In fact, John Stuart Mill used his essay "On Liberty" to make just such an argument—the argument that the religious toleration as developed by Locke should be extended to political toleration. Mill advocated for individual liberty of thought, speech, and action as necessary components for individual and societal development as well as for the defense of and promulgation of truth. For Mill, the only plausible limit of toleration for liberty (thought, speech, and action) was when, and only when, one's use of liberty brought direct and unavoidable severe harm to others. The toleration Mill argued for, of course, went beyond religious toleration to encompass political toleration. But it went still further than that. Mill's arguments for liberty and his writings on toleration were meant to be applied to social, as well as political and religious, aspects of life. It was so broad as to be all encompassing. In contrast to Locke who argued for toleration based on a theory of individual natural rights, Mill argued for toleration on purely utilitarian grounds. For twenty-first century America, Mill's conception of toleration, arguably a masterpiece of liberal polemic, is the basis of the political tolerance that has become such an important virtue of liberal democracy.

Political Tolerance and Prejudice

Tolerance is not interchangeable or synonymous with a lack of prejudice. Tolerance is about enduring what a citizen holds up to be objectionable or disagreeable; tolerance presumes disagreement. According to Sullivan, Piereson, and Marcus (1982, 4), "We sometimes say a person without prejudice is very tolerant, while those who are prejudiced are necessarily intolerant. Yet this need not be so. The prejudiced person may in fact be tolerant, if he understands his prejudices and proceeds to permit the expression of those things toward which he is prejudiced." Nunn et al. (1978, 11) also argues that tolerance is not synonymous with a lack of prejudice: "One may hold to prejudices and still be willing to let other people have their opinions and beliefs. Or one may even have a relatively benign attitude toward a people of a particular ethnic background and yet frequently violate others' civil liberties." Sullivan et al. (1982) concisely highlights the distinction between prejudice and political tolerance:

> A "prejudiced" attitude is commonly said to combine (1) stereotyped beliefs about a group, (2) negative evaluations of the group, and (3) a predisposition to act negatively toward the group. It is sometimes argued, as noted, that the reverse of a "prejudiced" attitude is a "tolerant" one; the tolerant individual does not hold stereotyped beliefs or negative evaluations of groups and is generally disposed to act positive toward them. Jackman (1977) questions this view. Even if people hold generalized beliefs about other groups that lead to negative evaluations, it does not follow that such beliefs will lead to hostile actions. People may combine strong norms of tolerance with generally negative feelings about some groups, in which case they must be said to be prejudiced but tolerant. Thus, the prejudiced person may be either tolerant or intolerant, depending on what action he or she is prepared to take politically. Given our definition, in fact, the issue of tolerance or intolerance does not come into play unless one holds negative beliefs or evaluations about the group or doctrine in question (Sullivan et al. 1982, 5).

In general, prejudice is either an inappropriate or a negative value judgment of an individual or group of individuals that is not based upon fact but is rather a stereotyped generalization formed previously to any interaction with the individual or group. Gordon Allport (1954) developed a classic definition of prejudice by arguing that prejudice was an antipathy, based on incorrect and unchangeable generalizations, toward a group or individual from a specific group. Prejudice is, in short, a thought or an attitude. Therefore, prejudice does not imply tolerance or intolerance. Political tolerance depends on the actions taken in relationship to one's judgment (e.g., thoughts or attitudes) whether or not that person is prejudiced toward ideas, groups, or persons he or she is opposed to. Basically, tolerance and value agreement are not synonymous. Actually quite the opposite is true: When there is agreement on values, tolerance is not an issue or concern.

Limits of Political Tolerance

Arguably the most obvious and consequential limitation to political tolerance involves the debate and discussion about whether or not we are required to tolerate those things that would ultimately lead to the demise of liberal democracy. If political tolerance is the preeminent and most important virtue of liberal democracy, then are there no grounds on which intolerance is acceptable? In contrast, if political tolerance is only one virtue among many in a liberal democracy, there are indeed things that become acceptable for citizens to be intolerant about.

Tolerance, of course, should not be extended to every person in every circumstance. For example, an individual, who, out of a strong desire to be tolerant and nonjudgmental, stands by and watches a heinous assault being committed—doing nothing to stop it or call police when he or she has the ability to do so—could hardly be praised for being tolerant of the beliefs or actions of others, in this case a violent attacker (Stetson and Conti 2005, 142).

This is a straightforward example of other values, such as moral culpability, and how those values influence the condition under which tolerance or intolerance may be preferred among other values. Crick (1973, 64) subscribes to a similar view when he says tolerance ". . . is a value to be held among other values—such as justice, and liberty itself, but also order and truth; it can never always be right to be tolerant; there are occasions on which we should be intolerant."[1]

The answers produced in debate and discussion about the appropriate limit of political tolerance depend on the democratic theory used in defense of them. In characterizing representative democratic theory in contemporary America, the work of John Stuart Mill and John Locke has led to the argument that what tolerance best exemplifies is the freedom to enter and exit the marketplace of ideas. This freedom must be broadly protected because the only way to counter or eradicate intolerance is for the "right" or "good" to vigorously compete and ultimately prevail over other less desirable ideas. The assumption undergirding representative democratic theory is that human nature is sophisticated; therefore, given competition of ideas, the ideal of tolerance will prevail over intolerance. For those who subscribe to an elitist democratic theory, as represented in contemporary political thought by the work of Joseph Schumpeter (1950) and Walter Lippman (1955), only those with the requisite skills and abilities to govern are capable of practicing political tolerance. Therefore, intolerance is mitigated by the governance of the elites and the passivity of the masses (because, after all, the citizen masses are deemed incapable of practicing political tolerance). The assumption here is that elites have a sophisticated human nature while the masses do not. Finally, federalist democracy theory is best exemplified by the writings of James Madison who argued for divisions of government (both between the branches of government and between the levels of government) and the need for a plurality of "factions" to ensure against the tyranny of the majority (*Federalist* 51 and 10, respectively). Political tolerance is guaranteed through the structure of governmental institutions to ensure competition for power. In short, the constitutional structure and competing interests cause political tolerance to prevail over intolerance because tolerance is in the self-interest of the competing factions. The assumption of human nature in this theory is that all human nature is flawed or circumspect.[2] Political intolerance could only be an advantage when one faction attains absolute power over all the rest, resulting in political tyranny and the end of tolerance.

Consequently, the role of political tolerance is extremely important from the perspective of representative democratic theory, and therefore, limitations on it should be minimal. In contrast, within elitist democratic theory, the role of political tolerance is less important insofar as it is not expected that the mass citizenry is capable of exercising it. The logical conclusion is that if the governing elite deem some opinions dangerous to the survival of the society, then those opinions can be limited. Finally, federalist democracy theory relies neither upon the spread of a tolerant ideal among the citizens (as does representative democratic theory) nor does it rely on a sophisticated elite (as does elitist democratic theory), rather the theory relies on a diverse constitutional structure and numerous political interests to constrain political intolerance as a viable option. The argument is that there will be so many divisions of interests and opinions that no single interest or opinion will be able to dominate.[3] Ultimately, all empirical studies of political tolerance lead to an examination of the underlying democratic theories (and their related assumptions) on which the empirical models rest. Mine is no different.

Religion and Tolerance in the United States: Mapping the Deficiencies

The relationship between religion and political tolerance has been (and still is) studied in separate and distinct scholarly arenas (as it relates to the discipline of political science).[4] Although the analyses in the following chapters will bridge some of the gaps that such a situation inevitably creates, informing the reader of this situation must begin at the outset of the book. The project I undertake here is situated at the intersection of religion and politics and political tolerance scholarship. Both bodies of research are a necessary basis for my project.

It is also necessary that I position the analyses accurately in relation to others in these respective fields and be forthcoming in laying out the evidence against which I am arguing, because this book challenges the accepted orthodoxy as it relates to religion/religiosity and political tolerance. Past scholarly research casts more than mere aspersions on the influence of religion/religiosity in a liberal democracy, and I am arguing against nearly forty years of study that suggests not only that religion/religiosity is a threat to liberal democracy but that it produces attitudes inimical to fostering and sustaining a healthy liberal democracy. Although such a foundational exercise may appear to be a straightforward literature review, the tasks in this project represent much more.

Beginning with Stouffer's ([1955] 1992) seminal study "Communism, Conformity, and Civil Liberties: A Cross-Section of the Nation Speaks Its Mind," the weight of nearly four decades of empirical political tolerance scholarship bears heavily on the question of whether or not religiously committed individuals act in a politically tolerant manner. The research (including Erskine & Siegal 1975; Filsinger 1976; Nunn et al. 1978; Corbett 1982; Smidt & Penning 1982; Sullivan et al. 1982; Beatty & Walter 1984; and Wilcox & Jelen 1990) suggests that the answer is "no." Given the record of results, I nevertheless advance the argument that the religion/religiosity of individuals in the contemporary United States is not the threat to liberal democracy that research and popular perception have declared.

I advance my argument on three fronts: empirical limitations, recent theoretical developments that have not been fully explored in the literature, and practical political and sociological considerations. The empirical limitations are brought into full view through a brief review of the extant political tolerance literature, I integrate the mainstream political tolerance literature—vis-à-vis the religion and politics literature that addresses political tolerance—and discuss how the relationships and linkages between religion and political tolerance have not been carefully examined. This is followed by a discussion of the other two fronts on which I advance my argument—recent theoretical developments that have not been fully explored and practical political and sociological considerations.

Extant Political Tolerance Literature and Its Empirical Limitations

The American political landscape is replete with the perceived incompatibility of our political ideals and our religious beliefs. Historically, this perceived inherent incompatibility rested on the idea that the very action of expressing religious belief required an individual to be intolerant of other individuals of dissimilar beliefs. The perception was that religion is about absolutes and liberal democratic politics is about compromise and tolerance (i.e., being a gracious loser); therefore, it was impossible to practice both in the same arena.[5] Also, liberal democratic politics was for the public arena and religion was for the private arena. Such a perception does not appear all that unreasonable. After all, religion tends to deal in absolutes whereby a set of truths delineates good from evil and facts from lies. To compromise with what one truly believes is evil or false is a steep demand.

> Because they do not lend themselves so readily to compromise solutions, religious issues may challenge the normal system of governance. If you regard abortion as murder, and I see it as a neutral medical procedure, it will be hard to find a middle ground that either one of us will accept as a legitimate public policy. . . . The same kind of problem may arise in the context of debates over prayer in public schools, the rights of homosexuals, traditional sex

> roles, and other policy areas in which religious groups have been active. . . . As religious issues do not easily permit compromise solutions, so, too, religious values may produce rigidity, dogmatism, and contempt for alternative points of view. Such destructive traits, far from being accidental, may actually be the consequence of religious commitment (Wald 1997, 321).

And modern empirical research appears to substantiate the connection between religion and political intolerance.

One of the first major studies of American attitudes toward civil liberties (or tolerance) was done by Stouffer ([1955] 1992). Using a format that would be replicated many times in the future, Stouffer obtained data from a national sample conducted in 1954. In it, respondents were asked about their willingness to extend various forms of freedoms to communists, socialists, and atheists; specifically, their willingness to let such a person teach in a college or university or give a speech in their community and whether they were willing to allow a book written by such a person to be housed in the public library.

Stouffer's seminal study supported a link between religious commitment (e.g., behavior) and intolerance and suggested that individuals who attended church regularly were less tolerant than those who attended irregularly or not at all. Twenty-eight percent of individuals who indicated that they had attended church in the last month fell into the "more tolerant" category. In contrast, 36 percent of individuals who indicated that they were nonattendees fell into this category (Stouffer [1955] 1992, 142, 144). Stouffer also uncovered differences among religious affiliations (e.g., religious belonging). Southern protestants, for example, had the lowest levels of tolerance with only 21 percent falling into the "more tolerant" category when combining church attendees and nonattendees. The tolerance level of northern protestants and Catholics was similar and occupied the middle ground (neither the most tolerant nor the least tolerant). Finally, although Stouffer cautioned that there was not a large enough sample of Jewish respondents to draw empirically substantive comparisons, he did note that Jewish respondents tended to be far more tolerant than both Catholics and protestants (Stouffer [1955] 1992, 142–43). These results held up under various control variables related to religion that might independently reduce political tolerance.

Stouffer's study did include religious tradition (a measure of belonging) and a measure for religious commitment (a measure of behavior), but the study relied on simple bivariate correlations, even when using control variables, between religious commitment and political tolerance, and the religious tradition categories were limited to protestant (northern/southern), Catholic, Jewish, Other, and None. In contrast, the work of Kellstedt and Green (1993), Layman (1997), Layman and Green (1998), and Steensland et al. (2000) provides a much better understanding and a more nuanced view of religious denominations within various religious traditions.[6] For example, we now know that a distinction exists between mainline Protestantism and evangelical Protestantism, which is something not incorporated in earlier studies, including Stouffer's.

In another comprehensive study, Nunn, Crockett, and Williams (1978) concluded that there is a negative link between religion and tolerance. These researchers based their data upon a 1973 survey. In order to map changes in political tolerance over the previous two decades, their study repeated the Stouffer items. Regarding the relationship between religion and tolerance, the evidence remained similar to that presented two decades earlier by Stouffer.[7] First, the rank order of tolerance among the religious versus nonreligious remained. Replicating the 1954 data, the Nunn, Crockett, and Williams results showed that 28 percent of the protestants, 31 percent of the Catholics, 71 percent of the Jews, and 49 percent of the individuals with no religious affiliation fell into the "more tolerant" category (Nunn et al. 1978, 129). The results from the 1973 survey showed that 46 percent of the protestants, 59 percent of the Catholics, 88 percent of the Jews, and 87 percent of the individuals with no religious affiliation fell into the "more tolerant" category. Nunn et al. (1978, 140) concluded that intolerance is built into the very nature of religious commitment.

Similar to Stouffer's work the Nunn et al. study was confined to the same limited denominational categories. In addition, in their "Multiple Classification Analysis" that controlled for education, gender, size of residence, age, and participation in voluntary associations, Nunn, Crockett, and Williams (1978, 140) measured religious commitment by a single measure that combined doctrinal belief (such as belief in the devil) and frequency of church attendance. Thus, what we now know to be two distinct measures of religiosity—belief and behavior—were combined in the 1978 study.

The next groundbreaking work on political tolerance was produced by Sullivan, Piereson, and Marcus (1982). In this seminal work, the authors successfully argued for a content-controlled (e.g., least-liked) measure of political tolerance,[8] and they also rigorously defined and causally modeled the social, psychological, and political predictors of political tolerance. These scholars also demonstrated a substantial difference between those with a denominational attachment versus the nonreligious; the nonreligious were far more likely to fall into the "more tolerant" category (44 percent) whereas only about 12 percent of protestants, Catholics, and Jews could be classified as "more tolerant" (Sullivan et al. 1982, 137–39).[9] In addition, they found little difference in tolerance levels between the various religious denominations. In the end, they concluded that religion was important insofar as one had a denominational attachment versus no attachment; the particular denominational attachment was of little consequence.

Nevertheless, there were several problems with the use of religion in their study. As with the research that preceded it, the religious tradition categories were limited (e.g., protestant, Catholic, Jewish, Other, and None) and in their analysis of various types of protestants (1982, 138), they use denominational classifications instead of a classification of the various denominations in broader religious traditions. The variable becomes even more imprecise when incorporated into their multivariate model in which religion is coded as Baptist/Other Religion/No Religion. Based on this tri-model variable, they conclude that "those from less traditional religions" have a more open personality and that the "less fundamentalist religious groups" are more liberal (1982, 222, 225). Such an imprecise measure cannot adequately distinguish between religious traditions. Furthermore, the "secular detachment" variable is a measure of sociological belonging (e.g., religious affiliation), not a measure of cognition (e.g., beliefs). Fundamentalism is more accurately defined as a specific theological belief or outlook (Marsden 1980), and it is more accurately measured by items tapping the level of doctrinal orthodoxy, such as beliefs about the Bible (Green et al. 1994; Layman 1997; Layman & Green 1998) or whether someone considers himself or herself "born-again" (Jelen 1991; Layman & Green 1998).

McCloskey and Brill (1983) produced a tour-de-force analysis of political tolerance in America. In their assessment of religion in relation to political tolerance (1983, chap. 8), they concluded that

Jews, Episcopalians, and those with no religious affiliation had the highest support for civil liberties, while Baptists scored the lowest (1983, 404, 405); the different religious affiliations they assessed were Jewish, Catholic, total protestant, Episcopalian, Lutheran, Methodist, Baptist, Presbyterian, other protestant sects, and none. These scholars also assessed support for civil liberties by what they called "religiosity," which was defined as "strength of religious conviction . . . the degree to which respondents value and rely upon religious beliefs and modes of explanation" (1983, 406). The results across all three of their data sets indicated that increased religiosity resulted in decreased support for civil liberties, and the trend remained the same even when controlling for education (1983, 406–11).

Once again, this study has some of the same problems associated with the measurement of religion as those that preceded it. McCloskey and Brill (1983) use denominational categories, which we now know are less useful than classifying respondents by religious tradition. There are also problems with the way in which McCloskey and Brill measured religious belief (what they called "religiosity"). The most common way in which religious believing is conceptualized is by doctrinal orthodoxy (or doctrinal beliefs). Typically, this can be measured by questioning individual beliefs regarding the literalism or inerrancy of the Bible (Leege & Kellstedt 1993; Layman & Green 1998). It can also be measured by tapping into the relationship between the individual and the divine by asking about the "born-again" experience. Many, if not most, of the questions used by McCloskey and Brill to measure religious believing did not address doctrinal orthodoxy at all (1983, 406).

A common problem with the political tolerance scholarship is that, all too often, religion is left out of the analysis altogether. Such is the case with Marcus et al. (1995), Gibson (1992), and Davis and Silver (2004). These are examples of scholarship by some of the most widely published and well-known scholars of political tolerance today (e.g., Marcus et al. 1995; Gibson 1992) as well as scholarship based on national samples (e.g., Gibson 1992; Davis & Silver 2004). Other studies that have addressed the role of religion in relation to political tolerance have deficiencies in the measurement of political tolerance as well as in appropriately specifying the determinants of political tolerance.

For various reasons (including the use of secondary data analysis), many of them could not employ the content-controlled tolerance measure developed by Sullivan, Piereson, and Marcus (e.g., Filsinger 1976; Smidt & Penning 1982; Beatty & Walter 1984; and Wilcox & Jelen 1990).[10] In addition, many of the political tolerance studies (including Cutler & Kaufman 1975; Davis 1975; Filsinger 1976; Smidt & Penning 1982; Beatty & Walter 1984; and Wilcox & Jelen 1990) did not incorporate two of the most important predictors of political tolerance: threat perception and support for norms of democracy (Sullivan et al. 1982; Marcus et al. 1995).[11] Also, they did not control for a secure personality,[12] which has been found to be an important psychological predictor of political tolerance (Sullivan et al. 1982; Davis 1995; Marcus et al. 1995; Peffley et al. 2001).

Green et al. (1994) is one of the best attempts to bring together religion, political tolerance, and important political predictors in a causal model. Nevertheless, the data for this study is focused solely on religious activists. In addition, some of the predictors of political tolerance used, such as the authors' Christian militancy scale, may be applicable solely to religious activists—the study categorized this variable as one of several political variables and argued that this variable was meant to assess a particular sample of the "political strata." At any rate, such a variable is not commonplace within the broad scope of the tolerance literature (e.g., Sullivan et al. 1982; Davis 1995; Marcus et al. 1995; Peffley et al. 2001). Furthermore, they include other predictors—political information and political participation—that have not received much support within the broader political tolerance literature. At the same time, the authors left out some of the most important predictors for political tolerance—support for the norms of democracy, threat perception, and secure personality (Sullivan et al. 1982; Marcus et al. 1995).

Theoretical Developments and Political/Social Considerations

In addition to the problems and limitations just discussed, the earlier empirical findings are at odds with contemporary theory regarding the relationship between religion/religiosity and modern democracy. According to Kraynak (2001, 1), within the American Christian community there is widespread agreement that "the form of government most compatible with the Christian religion is democracy." Democracy is a God-ordained style of governance that is to be preferred above other types of governance; although he later adds, "[t]oday's condition, where most Christian theologians and churches accept democratic politics, is a historical anomaly, a peculiarity of modern time" (2001, 3). Therefore, while the American founding fathers properly acquainted with the evils perpetrated by (or in the name of) religion across Europe had legitimate concerns about tolerance and thus the proper place for religion within a democratic decision-making process, the same does not hold true for contemporary American culture.

If Kraynak is correct and those within current American religious culture welcome "modern liberal democracy as a friend and an ally, even though they may criticize some of its features as misguided or downright immoral," then there is no reason to conclude that religion/religiosity per se fosters liberal democratic intolerance or that it is inimical to liberal democratic tolerance (2001, 167). In fact, Kraynak argues that "modern liberal democracy needs a religious basis because its moral claims cannot be vindicated by secular and rational means alone" even if that basis is derived from a revealed book and a tradition that has not been "necessarily liberal or democratic" (2001, xii, xiii).

Although the theoretical logic of the perspectives that have held sway against religion being compatible with the democratic value of tolerance since the writing of the American Constitution is understandable, this attribute of religion is not expected to be empirically consistent with modern religiosity nor is it expected that intolerance is empirically attributable primarily to religion or religious conviction. This is the case because the socialization of American liberal democratic values, which permeate religion in the United States, negates the European tradition of intolerance. Arguably, the very nature of religion has changed in the United States to make the religious individual neither more nor less tolerant than his or her less religious neighbor.

There is no way to understate this argument. The interaction between liberal democracy and American governance has produced a unique situation in which those most committed to their religion are not advocates of any other form of government than liberal democracy (they do not advocate theocracy as is often implied). They are proud supporters of American liberal democracy and very convinced that it is a better (more moral) form of government than other forms of government (e.g., the "godless" communists). The relationship between committed religious individuals in support of liberal democracy is not the same relationship between religion and government found in Old World Europe—the relationship that so vexed the American founding fathers that they sought to disestablish religion from the government and, at the same time, guarantee religious freedom. The experiment of democracy in the United States has created a situation in which the relationship between religion and government is qualitatively different than that which had existed for millennia.

Additionally, a natural political maturation of different religious sectors has emerged. The data collection for previous empirical survey studies occurred more than fifteen years ago. For example, Nunn et al. (1978) used data collected in 1973 and concluded that intolerance is built into the very nature of religious commitment. Wilcox and Jelen (1990) used that same data from 1973 and concluded that doctrinal orthodoxy plays a major role in the intolerance of evangelical protestants. Jelen (1991), using data collected in 1988, found an indication of a link between religious commitment and intolerance. The data from the late 1980s marks an important point in time. At that point, the reemergence of evangelical protestants into the public arena became institutionalized with the end of the Reagan presidency. Because evangelical protestants were already politically involved, this trend required Catholics and mainline protestants to either develop or learn tolerance as the modus operandi with this new political elephant. On the other hand, evangelical protestants found themselves as new actors on the political stage. With the increased involvement in modern politics of the various religious communities, along with Kraynak's arguments that Christian communities believe in democratic governance, I argue that we should expect findings, at a minimum, to begin to diverge from those culled from research using outdated data.

Finally, a shift has occurred in the educational demographic of religious communities. During the latter part of the twentieth century, an overall increase in the educational level of religious adherents (Greeley 1991) demonstrated that Catholic priests were no longer the most educated individuals in their churches. Marsden (1997) argues that evangelical protestants have made advances in educational attainment as well, although they still are likely to lag behind those of other religious traditions. Given the role of education as one of the primary agents in socializing citizens to support the norms of democratic behavior, we can expect religious individuals among the citizenry to possess socialized political values similar to nonreligious individuals.

Since Thomas Jefferson first argued for the logical and psychological incompatibility of religious orthodoxy and democratic decision-making, this has been an "accepted presupposition" of American democratic action and ideas of rights. However, it is important to challenge this "presupposition" by questioning whether the European religious orthodoxy that Thomas Jefferson recognized as problematic is qualitatively different from the religious orthodoxy in the contemporary United States. Bringing evidence to bear on this question, broadly speaking, is what the following chapters will facilitate. For a liberal democratic society, results contrary to the tightly held "presupposition" suggest that one need not be overly concerned that, by definition, religious individuals will act in a politically intolerant manner. Such findings may very well begin to free liberal democratic theory from the belief that religion is incompatible with commitment to liberal democratic ideals (particularly in terms of political tolerance).

Chapter 2

Christian Political Tolerance in Contemporary America

I also have this belief, strong belief, that freedom is not this country's gift to the world; freedom is the Almighty's gift to every man and woman in this world. And as the greatest power on the face of the Earth, we have an obligation to help the spread of freedom.

—*President George W. Bush, April 13, 2004*

In the previous chapter, I established the empirical limitations of the previous scholarship within mainstream political tolerance research as well as the religion and politics literature on political tolerance. Within the mainstream political tolerance scholarship, many studies have not addressed the role of religion (Cutler & Kaufman 1975; Davis 1975; Marcus et al. 1995) and have used measures of religion/religiosity that are less rigorous than desired, given the methodological advances in this scholarly area (Nunn et al. 1978; Sullivan et al. 1982; Stouffer [1955] 1992). Within the religion and politics scholarship many studies have not incorporated some of the most sophisticated political tolerance measures—such as the content-controlled least-liked measure developed by Sullivan et al. (1982)—in the analysis (Smidt & Penning 1982; Beatty & Walter 1984; Wilcox & Jelen 1990). Furthermore, some studies have not included some or all of the psychological and political predictors explicated by Sullivan et al. (Beatty & Walter 1984; Wilcox & Jelen 1990; Green et al. 1994). Still others have used statistical techniques less rigorous than Structural Equation Modeling.

In the preceding chapter, I also highlighted the limitation of theoretical developments regarding religion and political tolerance as it pertains to liberal democracy that has not been fully explored in the literature and the limitations of previous scholarship resulting from political and demographic changes of religious individuals across the American landscape. I argue that these limitations and deficiencies have led to empirical results that cast a gray cloud over the influence of religion/religiosity in modern America. I argue further that a new assessment addressing the empirical limitations of previous scholarship will produce results that diverge from the scholarship that highlights a negative relationship between religion/religiosity and political tolerance. In this chapter,[1] therefore, the primary purpose is to empirically reexamine the validity of the claim that religion/religiosity leads individuals toward intolerance. This chapter will not explain the existing determinants of political tolerance—these are well established in the literature. Rather, the analysis, exposition, and discussion supporting my argument focus solely on the connection between the political tolerance scholarship and the mainstream religion and politics scholarship.

A New Beginning

In the broadest sense, religion refers to a belief in the existence of a transcendental universal reality beyond that which is evidenced by our empirical observation. Because this "reality" is transcendental and universal, humans do not have a direct sensory experience with it. Consequently, there must be some component of "faith"—a belief that a reality outside this world exists and that it functions outside of human control.

> When they have contemplated the world, human beings have always experienced a transcendence and mystery at the heart of existence. They have felt that it is deeply connected with themselves and with the natural world, but that it also goes beyond. However we choose to define it—it has been called God, Brahma, or Nirvana—this transcendence has been a fact of human life. We have all experienced something similar, whatever our theological opinions, when we listen to a great piece of music or hear a beautiful poem and feel touched within and lifted, momentarily, beyond ourselves. (Armstrong 1996, xvi)

However, such definitions of religion do not lend themselves to empirical analyses and cannot be evaluated directly. Given this, religion typically is defined by the "manner and form in which religious phenomena appear in human existence" (Capps 1972, 135); that is, defined by behavior (e.g., church attendance), religious affiliation (e.g., denomination or tradition), a particular set of religious beliefs (e.g., doctrinal or theological beliefs), or a combination of the three.

In reexamining the linkage between religion/religiosity and political tolerance, I bring together four important elements:

1. The least-liked (or content-controlled) political tolerance measure developed by Sullivan, Piereson, and Marcus (1982).
2. Doctrinal orthodoxy (belief), religious tradition (belonging), and religious commitment (behavior)[2] in the development of a religious model of political tolerance.
3. Important political and psychological predictors of political tolerance explicated in the work of Sullivan et al. (1982).
4. Structural equation modeling, allowing for maximum understanding of the linkage between these variables.[3]

Given the findings from scholarly research presented in chapter 1, I advance three potential explanations regarding the relationship between religion/religiosity and political tolerance. The first explanation is that religious commitment (e.g., behavior) may lead to increased intolerance. Second, higher levels of doctrinal orthodoxy or orthodox beliefs (what Sullivan et al. [1982] call "fundamentalism") may lead to increased intolerance. Both of these hypotheses are well supported by a bevy of past research (Stouffer [1955] 1992; Nunn et al. 1978; Smidt & Penning 1982; Sullivan et al. 1982; Beatty & Walter 1984; and Wilcox & Jelen 1990); therefore, these are the findings that one should expect. The third explanation is that the relationship between religion/religiosity and political tolerance is spurious because once religion/religiosity is causally modeled using a content-controlled measure of political tolerance and incorporating important political and psychological predictors of tolerance, the relationship frequently reported between religiosity and intolerance will not manifest. In light of Kraynak's (2001) theoretical arguments, this outcome is not just possible but probable. The following analysis will first deal with the first and third explanations and will then assess the second explanation (regarding doctrinal orthodoxy). This is done for reasons that will be explained within the body of the analysis.

The Data for the Analysis

The data for this chapter comes from a random sample phone survey of 601 individuals in Lake County, Indiana, conducted specifically for this project. With the data presented coming from a single county within a single state, the inevitable questions will arise as to how generalizations can be made effectively and accurately. But an argument can be made that this sampling is representative of "middle America," and therefore, one can reasonably conclude that religiosity and political tolerance in one Midwestern county will not be radically different from the religiosity and political tolerance in another Midwestern county. Nevertheless, the sample size of 601 is smaller than desired, which also raises the question of generalizability. While the sampling size clearly is a drawback, it is equally clear that the data obtained is based on a random sample of adequate size and, at a minimum, means that the findings certainly can be considered suggestive even though they cannot be deemed conclusive.

The Indiana University Public Opinion Laboratory, which is located on the campus of Indiana University-Purdue University Indianapolis (IUPUI), collected the telephone survey data. The phone survey was administered using random-digit dialing (done by randomly generating the last two digits of telephone numbers). Interviews with Lake County residents were conducted between August 7 and August 25, 2003. All phone calls were made between 4:00 p.m. and 9:30 p.m. (CST). The interviews lasted approximately 14 to 15 minutes. Respondents were chosen within each household by asking to speak to the adult, 18 years of age or older, who had the most recent birthday. All interview breakoffs and refusals were recontacted at least once to convert respondent to a completed interview.[4]

In the 2000 census, the population of Lake County, Indiana (persons who were 18 years of age and older), was 354,767 out of a total population of 484,564. Table 2.1 shows these basic demographics in my data set. Overall, the racial makeup of Lake County (regardless of age) is 66.7 percent white, 25.3 percent black, 12.2 percent Latino/Hispanic, and .08 percent Asian. In addition, the county (regardless of age) is 51.8 percent female and 48.2 percent male. Of the 601 respondents in my data set, 46.6 percent (280) are male and 53.4 percent are female (321). The racial makeup of my data set is 72.4 percent white (435), 15.1 percent black (91), 9.9 percent Latino/Hispanic (60), 0.5 percent Asian (3), 0.2 percent Native American (1), and 0.7 percent bira-

Table 2.1

Demographics of My Data Set vs County Data					
	My Data	*County Data*		*My Data*	*County Data*
	Sex/Gender	*Sex/Gender*		*Race*	*Race*
Male	46.6% (280)	48.2%	*White*	72.4% (435)	66.7%
Female	53.4% (321)	51.8%	*Black*	15.1% (91)	25.3%
			Latino/ Hispanic	9.9% (60)	12.2%
			Asian	0.5% (3)	0.8%
			American Indian	0.2% (1)	
			Bi/Multi Racial	0.7% (4)	
			No Ans.	1.2% (7)	
TOTAL	100% (601)	100%		100% (601)	

cial or multiracial (4). The remainder (1.2 percent) did not provide answers.

The Model for the Analysis

Figure 2.1 presents a religious model of political tolerance. This model and all the pertinent concepts (except for the religion variables) are derived primarily from the work of Sullivan, Piereson, and Marcus (1982) and Marcus et al. (1995). Of particular interest and focus for this section is the direct influence of religious commitment on political tolerance. Previous research (Stouffer [1955] 1992; Nunn et al. 1978; Smidt & Penning 1982; Beatty & Walter 1984; and Wilcox & Jelen 1990) suggests that religious commitment directly influences political tolerance so that as commitment increases political tolerance decreases.

Figure 2.1
BASIC RELIGIOUS MODEL OF POLITICAL TOLERANCE

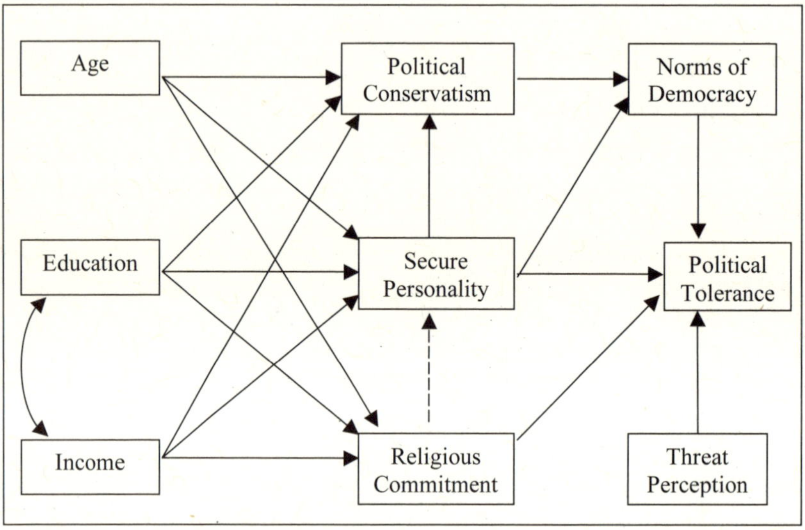

In figure 2.1,[5] the relationship between religious commitment and a secure personality is shown with the dashed line (---). It is generally accepted that religious commitment has the capability of influencing political attitudes and that this influence is most likely a conservative one (Smidt & Penning 1982; Beatty & Walter 1984; Wilcox 1987; Wilcox & Jelen 1990; Green et al, 1994; Layman 1997; Layman & Green 1998). Drawing across this work as well as political tolerance research, the general conclusion is that religion/religiosity contributes to attitudes or beliefs that are less likely to allow for acceptance of ideas among those who disagree. Given this, I have modeled a path between religious commitment and a secure personality because one of the components of a secure personality is dogmatism (e.g., open or closed mind). Finally, religious tradition is not depicted visually in the model but is a component of analysis, and its inclusion is fully explained in the analyses given later in the chapter.

Measurement of Variables

The model presented in figure 2.1 requires the use of multiple variables. What follows is an explanation of how each variable in the model is measured for inclusion.

Political Tolerance

This research has adopted the content-controlled or least-liked measurement approach developed by Sullivan et al. (1982). This approach requires that respondents be allowed to identify their most disliked group from among a list of "extremist" groups that represent the right as well as the left, in addition to groups that do not necessarily fall on the left-right continuum. If their most disliked group is not on the list, respondents are asked to name the group. They are then asked to respond to a series of five statements about "a range of peaceful activities in which members of that group might participate or about steps the government might take against that group" (Sullivan et al. 1982, 61) to measure political tolerance (Sullivan et al. 1982; Davis 1995; Marcus et al.). Respondents were asked each tolerance statement listed in table 2.2. Each statement has a five-point scale ranging from strongly agree (1) to strongly disagree (5).

> It should be emphasized that the activities referred to in these questions—such as running for office, teaching in the public schools, holding a rally, and making a public speech—are all peaceful in nature and otherwise perfectly legal and constitutional. Since tolerance refers to the willingness to permit the peaceful expression of ideas that one rejects, it was necessary to measure it in connection with activities that are legal and constitutional. (Sullivan et al. 1982, 62)

Table 2.2

Content-Controlled Political Tolerance Scale Items

Item 1	Members of the (subject selected least-liked group) should be banned from running for public office in the United States.
Item 2	Members of the (subject selected least-liked group) should be allowed to teach in public schools.
Item 3	The (subject selected least-liked group) should be outlawed.
Item 4	Members of the (subject selected least-liked group) should be allowed to make a public speech.
Item 5	The (subject selected least-liked group) should be allowed to hold public rallies.

Although challenges to the "least-liked" measurement approach for tolerance (e.g., Mueller 1988; Gibson 1992) have been made, they have not been compelling enough to invalidate the use of this approach. For example, Mueller (1988) suggests that tolerance does not require a strong dislike. Furthermore, he suggests that there may be more than one type of intolerance. He argues that intolerance may result from a strong dislike or opposition or that intolerance may result from the perceived threat that a group represents (18). Similarly, Gibson (1992) argues that some respondents may name more "trivial" groups, while others will name groups that are perceived as more threatening. Thus, the dislike of the threatening group will be more intense than the dislike of the "trivial" group (575). For example, although a person may strongly dislike *Earth First!* activists, he or she may not view them as a threat to the established social order or to governmental functioning. Therefore, the person will be more likely to be tolerant of them, even though he or she may strongly dislike them.

This line of reasoning is not considered compelling because, while it is true that threat perception is important for predicting tolerance, threat perception can be—and typically is—controlled for in tolerance scholarship by its inclusion as a predictor of political tolerance (Sullivan et al. 1982; Sullivan et al. 1993; Davis 1995; Marcus et al. 1995; Peffley et al. 2001). Furthermore, the need to control for threat perception remains present even when other measures of tolerance are used, such as the standard and widely employed General Social Surveys (GSS) measures. It is important to note that Gibson, who initially was a critic of the least-liked tolerance measurement approach (e.g., Gibson 1986; Gibson 1989), has changed his position. After empirically testing both the GSS and least-liked measurement approaches, he concluded that both measurement strategies were equally effective. Although he still voiced reservations about the least-liked method, he nonetheless suggested that the least-liked method was more amenable over time. Since then, Gibson has embraced the least-liked measurement strategy in his own research (e.g., Gibson & Gouws 2000 and Sullivan et al. 1993, of which Gibson is one of the coauthors.)

Secure Personality

Secure personality is measured by two traits: dogmatism and self-esteem (Sullivan et al. 1982; Davis 1995; Marcus et al. 1995; Peffley et al. 2001). Dogmatism refers to rigidity of mind or rigidity of thought.

A "closed mind" is unwilling to consider alternative views, in contrast to an "open mind" that is willing to consider ideas that are different from one's own (Rokeach 1960). Self-esteem refers to our self-attitudes, whether good or bad. It can be thought of as personal (un)worthiness (Sniderman 1975). Dogmatism is measured with two items (Sullivan et al. 1982; Davis 1995; Marcus et al. 1995). They are: (1) There are two kinds of people in this world—those who are for the truth and those who are against the truth; and (2) Most of the ideas which get printed nowadays aren't worth the paper they are printed on. Each item has five response categories ranging from strongly agree (1) to strongly disagree (5). Self-esteem is measured with three True (coded 1) or False (coded 5) response items (Peffley et al. 2001). They are: (1) I am certainly lacking in self-confidence; (2) I doubt whether I would make a good leader; and (3) It is hard for me to start a conversation with strangers.

Political Conservatism

Typically, political conservatism is measured with a seven-point scale, ranging from extremely liberal (1) to extremely conservative (7); for a phone survey the format is slightly varied. Respondents are asked: In politics today, do you think of yourself as a conservative (coded 1), as middle of the road (coded 2), as a liberal (coded 3), or do you not think of yourself in these terms (coded 4)?

Norms of Democracy

Norms of democracy refers to expressions of support for abstract liberal democratic principles. It can include support for general norms of a liberal democracy (e.g., free speech and legal rights) as well as procedural norms of a democracy (e.g., majority vote, release on bail, the right to not be forced to testify against oneself). This study specifically measures support for general norms of liberal democracy. Two items, ranging from strongly agree (1) to strongly disagree (5), are used to measure support for norms of democracy (Sullivan et al. 1993). They are: (1) No matter what a person's political beliefs are, he is entitled to the same legal rights and protections as anyone else; (2) I believe in free speech for all no matter what their views might be.

Both of the items measuring support for norms of democracy have little variability. Item 1 has a standard deviation of .859 (94.5

percent of all respondents agree or strongly agree with this item), while the standard deviation for item 2 is .744 (88.8 percent of all respondents agree or strongly agree with this item). The responses for these items are skewed toward high support for norms of democracy. This is not unusual or unexpected. Americans have consistently demonstrated considerable support of democratic norms when asked about them in the abstract (Protho & Grigg 1960; McClosky 1964; Sullivan et al. 1982; McClosky & Brill 1983).

Threat Perception

Threat perception is intended to capture the perception of an objectionable group's strength and, therefore, its potential to endanger important values or social or constitutional order, as they are perceived by the respondent. Respondents are asked to rate their "least-liked" group by one adjective pair—"safe/dangerous"—ranging from very safe to very dangerous. Respondents are asked whether they would describe their least-liked group as safe or dangerous. Answers range from very safe, somewhat safe to very dangerous, and somewhat dangerous.

Religious Commitment

Religious commitment is measured by frequency of attendance (at a religious institution), frequency of personal prayer, and religious salience (Kellstedt, Green, Guth & Smidt 1996; Layman & Green 1998). Although religious salience is an attitudinal variable, in the empirical measurement of religious commitment, scholars typically also include the subjective salience of religion question (e.g., the National Election Survey [NES] question regarding the amount of guidance religion provides) under religious "behaving" (Guth & Green 1993; Kellstedt 1993).[6]

Doctrinal Orthodoxy

Doctrinal orthodoxy is measured by a single variable, biblical literalism, which in turn has three response categories ranging from most orthodox to least orthodox. The exact question wording is: Which of these statements comes closest to describing your feelings about the Bible? The Bible is the actual word of God and is to be taken literally, word for word (this is classified as high orthodoxy). The Bible is the inspired word of God but not everything in it should be taken literally, word for word (this is classified as medium orthodoxy). The Bible is an ancient book of fables, legends, history, and moral precepts recorded by men (this is classified as low orthodoxy).

Religious Tradition

Six religious traditions (minimal) are included in the religious tradition classification: evangelical protestant, mainline protestant, black protestant, Roman Catholic, Jewish, and secular (or the nonreligious) (Kellstedt & Green 1993; Layman & Green 1998; Steensland et al. 2000). Respondents are assigned to a specific religious tradition based on their answer to questions 15 and 16 in the survey questionnaire. For a review of the denominations classified into a particular religious tradition for this research, please review Kellstedt et al. (1996) and Steensland et al. (2000).

The remaining variables of education, age, and income are standard demographic variables. Exact question wording of items can be viewed in appendix A along with a brief discussion of limitations and assumptions of the data.

Target Group Selection

As stated previously, I employ the least-liked measurement strategy for political tolerance. Respondents must first select their least-liked group, then they are questioned about their willingness to extend civil liberties to that group. Therefore, it is of interest to find out the group or groups the respondents like the least. The least-liked measurement strategy allows respondents to select their own most disliked group and respondents are given an opportunity during the survey to choose a group not already mentioned as their most disliked, but most respondents selected the same few groups. Upon viewing the results in table 2.3, the percentage of respondents who chose the Ku Klux Klan as their most disliked group jumps off the page. The two next most likely targets are atheists and homosexuals. All combined, the Ku Klux Klan, atheists, and homosexuals account for 85.6 percent of all respondent choices.

Table 2.3

RESPONDENTS' LEAST-LIKED GROUP

Group	Percent
Socialists	2.3%
Ku Klux Klan	64.0%
Pro-Choice People	3.3%
Pro-Life People	1.3%
Atheists	15.3%
Homosexuals	6.3%
Religious Fundamentalists	3.3%
Feminists	0.2%
All Other Groups	4.0%
TOTAL	100% (562)

Although the choice of the Ku Klux Klan as the single most disliked group is high, it is not unprecedented. It is also consistent with past research. For example, in the seminal work by Sullivan, Piereson, and Marcus (1982), 38 percent of their respondents from a national survey conducted in 1978 selected the Ku Klux Klan as either their first or second most disliked group. In 1987, Gibson conducted a national survey using the "least-liked" measurement strategy and 61 percent of his respondents selected the Ku Klux Klan as either their first or second most disliked group. In fact, the Gibson study asked respondents to list their four most disliked groups, and 82.3 percent of the respondents selected the Ku Klux Klan as one of their four disliked groups.

In light of these results, three interesting caveats are worth mentioning. The fact that only three groups are selected by 85.6 percent of all respondents as their least-liked group appears to refute the theory of pluralistic intolerance in Sullivan et al. (1982). Also, the KKK is arguably an extreme right group; whereas, the original Stouffer items that were used to measure political tolerance have focused historically on the leftist nonconformist groups (the original Stouffer items are referring to the standard GSS survey items, which do not allow respondents to choose their least-liked group that historically have been used to measure political tolerance). Finally, the distribution of least-liked groups does provide minimal support for the Sullivan et al. (1982) contention that target groups are more dispersed across the ideological spectrum than earlier scholars had maintained.

Table 2.4

RESPONDENTS' LEAST-LIKED GROUP BY RELIGIOUS TRADITION

	Catholic	*Evangelical Protestant*	*Mainline Protestant*	*Secular*
Socialists	1.8%	1.6%	6.3%	0.0%
Ku Klux Klan	69%	58.2%	58.7%	80.6%
Pro-Choice People	4.8%	3.4%	3.3%	0.0%
Pro-Life People	2.5%	0.0%	1.7%	3.2%
Atheists	10.1%	23.8%	14.3%	9.7%
Homosexuals	6.0%	7.4%	7.9%	3.3%
Religious Fundamentalists	4.3%	0.0%	3.2%	6.3%
Feminists	0.0%	0.8%	0.0%	0.0%
All Other Groups	3.0%	4.9%	4.8%	3.2%

The target distribution is certainly limited to a few key groups, but most important for my purposes is whether or not target group selection differs by religious tradition. As shown in table 2.4, all four religious traditions choose as "least-liked" the Ku Klux Klan more than half of the time. This is not surprising given the previous results. However, the secular group is dramatically more likely to choose this group as their least-liked. After that, atheists are the second largest target group. Evangelical protestants are particularly likely to choose atheists as their least-liked. It is interesting that even the secular group chooses atheists as its least-liked target group (9.7 percent).

It is also interesting to note that none in the secular group chose pro-choice people as their most-disliked group, and no evangelical protestants chose pro-life people as their most disliked group. To give credit where credit is due, Catholics and mainline protestants are willing to choose pro-life people as their most disliked group. Not every Catholic or mainline protestant is necessarily pro-life, but most of the religious institutions that these individuals are likely to belong to condemn the practice. As a point of general information, the groups chosen that were classified "All Other Groups" in the previous two tables is quite an interesting assortment. The list includes liars, the Nation of Islam, Jehovah Witnesses, the ACLU, Arabs, anti-religious people, liberals, gang members, Episcopalians, gun control activists, racists, communists, Mexicans, Nazis/Neo-Nazis, Republicans, and politicians.

Unique Attributes of Data Set

As can be seen from table 2.5, evangelical protestants in this sample are much more likely to be Democrat than Republican.[7] Given the fact that this sampling is from Lake County, Indiana, this is not that difficult to explain and is consistent with the political behavior of the sampled population as a whole. Lake County is a heavy Democrat stronghold. East Chicago has, arguably the last remaining "machine" government run by the Democrats. In East Chicago, Gary, Highland, Hammond, Dyer, Schererville, Griffith, Merrillville and other cities in Lake County, it is difficult to win an elected office as a Republican. This is possibly because of the fact that Northwest Indiana has been defined, predominately, as a blue-collar manufacturing and industrial workforce population. For example, the heart of the steel industry resides in this area of the United States, which means that labor unions are still prominent in Northwest Indiana.

Table 2.5

Political Party by Religious Tradition

PARTY	*Democrat*	*Independent*	*Republican*	*Total*
Catholic	53.4% (102)	13.6% (26)	33.0% (63)	100% (191)
Evangelical Protestant	40.2% (45)	34.8% (39)	25.0% (28)	100% (112)
Mainline Protestant	29.3% (29)	13.1% (13)	57.6% (57)	100% (99)
Secular	45.9% (28)	31.1% (19)	23.0% (14)	100% (61)
Black Protestant	91.2% (52)	3.5% (2)	5.3% (3)	100% (57)

As an example of the Democratic dominance in Lake County, Indiana, a couple simple examples will suffice. In all the mayoral races[8] held in Lake County during the May 2003 primary, 89.9 percent of the votes were for Democrats out of 57,284 overall votes cast; that is, 51,524 votes were for Democrats and only 5,761 votes were for Republicans (representing 11.1 percent of the total votes cast). Furthermore, the town councils and mayors in Merrillville, Gary, Highland, Hammond, Whiting, and East Chicago, currently, are 100 percent Democrat.

Results

The results from the model just presented are shown in figure 2.2. This model is for all respondents without distinction between religious traditions. All path coefficients in bold print indicate significance at .05 or lower, and all estimates are the standardized estimates. For my purposes here, the most important findings are those related to explanations one and three—posited earlier—as well as the relationship indicated with dashed lines (---) in figure 2.1. The first explanation—increased religious commitment leads to increased political intolerance—cannot be supported. Instead of increased religious commitment leading to decreased tolerance, figure 2.2 shows a nominal increase in political tolerance with a path coefficient of .10 (p .08).

Figure 2.2

MODEL RESULTS FOR ALL RESPONDENTS

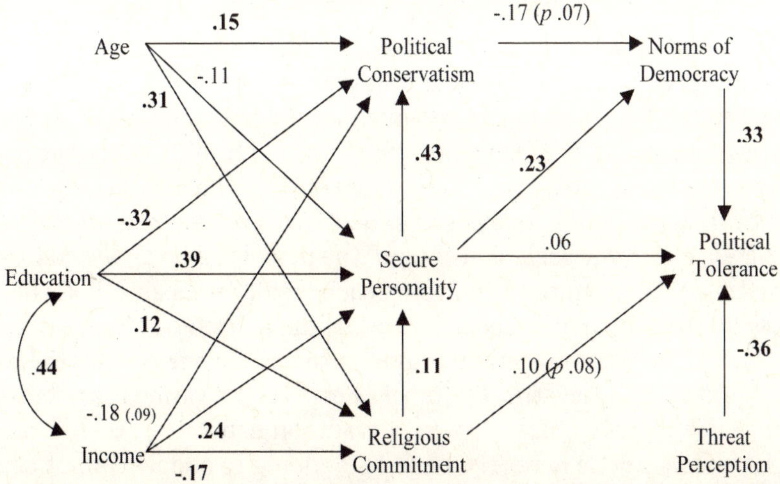

Thus, my third explanation is supported, which posits that the unmediated or direct relationship between religious commitment and political tolerance demonstrated in past research is spurious. Furthermore, religious commitment demonstrates no indirect negative influence on political tolerance either. This is important because one of the two components of a secure personality is dogmatism (e.g., open versus closed mind; the other component is self-esteem). Therefore, as religious commitment increases, an individual is not more likely to have a closed mind and decreased levels of self-esteem. The finding that differs from past research is the influence of education on religious commitment. Although the path coefficient is a weak one (.12), it is statistically significant and in the opposite direction of past research findings.

I am not attempting to reassess the predictors of political tolerance that are well established in the literature, but some of the other path coefficients are worth a mention. Both of the political predictors of political tolerance, threat perception, and support for norms of democracy demonstrate consistency with past research (Sullivan et al. 1982; Marcus et al. 1995). Increased support for norms of democracy leads to an increase in political tolerance, while increased levels of threat perception leads to a decrease in political tolerance. A preliminary conclusion from the results here is that when one is attempting to understand the influences on political intolerance, religion is not the place to look. Rather, political and psychological predictors are far more important.

The Religious Traditions

The results so far focus on a religious model of political tolerance without distinguishing between the various religious traditions. Now I turn to an analysis of the same model presented in figure 2.1; however, I will present results for each religious tradition separately. In essence, I am controlling for religious tradition. Religious tradition can be included in the analysis in two different ways. First, it can be included as dummy variables; second, the model can be analyzed for each tradition separately. Analyzing each tradition separately is the more interesting analysis because by looking at each tradition separately, we can assess whether or not variables change across traditions and we can view the differences between the various variables across the models. Analyzing each tradition separately, therefore, is the analysis done here. The benefits of doing so simply cannot be achieved when religious tradition is included as a dummy variable. If religious tradition were included in the model (fig. 2.1) as dummy variables, it would have to assume that the only variable that changes across tradition is the dependent variable, political tolerance.

In figure 2.3, the path coefficients are shown for four religious traditions: secular, Catholic, mainline protestant, and evangelical protestant. All coefficients are the standardized estimates, and all coefficients in bold print indicate significance at .05 or better. To delineate the estimates for each tradition, S is for secular, C is for Catholic, M is for mainline protestant, and E is for evangelical protestant. The sample size for secular is 95, Catholic is 219, evangelical protestant 120, and mainline protestant 99. Please note: Other religious traditions, such as Jewish and black protestant, are not included because the sample size was limited to 601 and there were not enough black protestants or Jewish respondents for inclusion.[9] I present figure 2.3 in two parts. Part A depicts the results for all variables in the model with the exception of demographic variables (age, education, and income). In Part B, the results are depicted for age, education, and income. I present the results in two parts to simplify the presentation of the data and to make it easier to read and understand. However, the model was estimated, as figure 2.1 depicts, as a single structural equation model in which all parameter estimates were obtained at one time, not in two different stages.

Figure 2.3A

MODEL RESULTS BY RELIGIOUS TRADITION

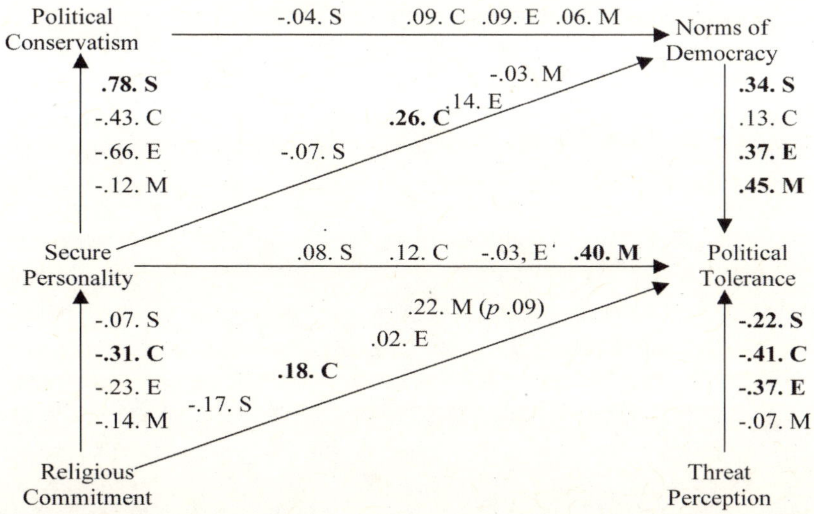

A quick look at figure 2.3A shows that, once again, there is no support for the first explanation posited at the beginning of this chapter (increased religious commitment will lead to increased political intolerance). For the evangelical protestant tradition, the relationship is nonexistent; for Catholics, increased religious commitment leads to more—not less—political tolerance; even the mainline protestant result is counter to the hypothesis with increased commitment leading to increased tolerance. This path coefficient is not statistically significant at .05 or less, with a *p* value of .09, but this should be given consideration because the mainline protestant model has a modest sample size of 99 respondents. The only religious tradition showing that increased commitment leads to increased intolerance is a statistically insignificant coefficient for seculars. Therefore, similar to the results from figure 2.2, for each religious tradition my third explanation—spuriousness—is supported. For the other relationship of interest, increased religious commitment does lead to a less secure personality for all four religious traditions (although only the parameter estimate for Catholics is statistically significant).

One interesting finding is the relationship between education and religious commitment (fig. 2.3B). The influence of education on religious commitment is positive rather than negative (similar to the results shown in figure 2.2), which is contrary to expectations from previous research. As can been seen from the results in figure 2.3B, the relationship between education and religious commitment is again contrary to what previous scholarship would lead us to expect. Increased education leads to increased religious commitment for both evangelical protestants and mainline protestants (the *p* value of .10 for mainline protestants is arguably significant given its smaller sample of 99). This finding might be perceived as more explicable for the mainline protestant tradition, but for the evangelical tradition, there is typically an anti-intellectual bias that this finding challenges.

Figure 2.3B
MODEL RESULTS BY RELIGIOUS TRADITION

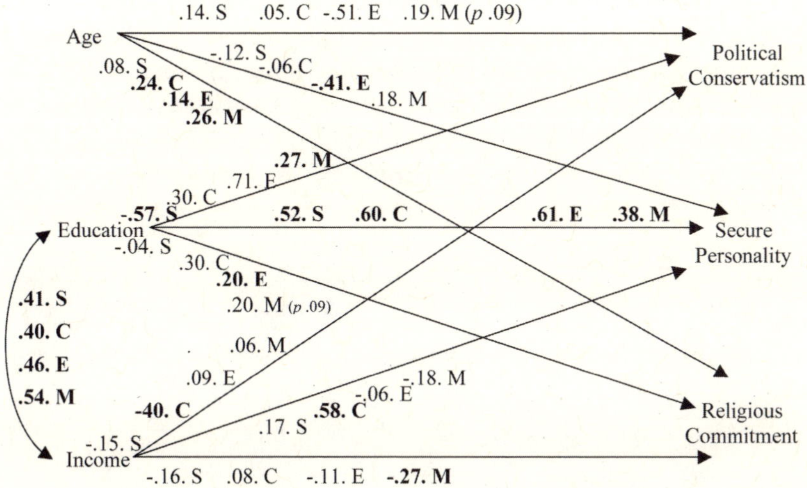

The Role of Doctrinal Orthodoxy

The preceding discussion focused on the relationship between religious commitment and political tolerance, but this section will look specifically at the influence of doctrinal orthodoxy on political tolerance. The reason for looking at doctrinal orthodoxy separate from the previous analyses is a pragmatic one. In the sample used to conduct these analyses, individuals classified as secular were not asked the doctrinal orthodoxy question asked of those classified into one of the Christian traditions. Therefore, while the preceding results could show differences across four traditions, including the secular group, this analysis cannot.

Previous research suggests that as doctrinal orthodoxy increases so does political intolerance (Wilcox & Jelen 1990). Therefore, in figure 2.4, a path is modeled between doctrinal orthodoxy and political tolerance. Two other relationships important to this model are shown with a dashed line (---). The two relationships are the influence of doctrinal orthodoxy on religious commitment, and the influence of doctrinal orthodoxy on threat perception. According to Wilcox and Jelen (1990), fundamentalism (referenced here as doctrinal orthodoxy) leads to increased levels of perceived threat. Also, in the words of Layman and Green (1998, 2), "Believing is the central motivation for religious belonging and behaving, and is made up of cognitions about the nature of the divine and humankind's relationship to it" (Leege & Kellstedt 1993). Drawing on these studies, I model a path between doctrinal orthodoxy (belief) and religious commitment (behavior) as well as a path between doctrinal orthodoxy and threat perception.

Figure 2.4
ADVANCED MODEL OF POLITICAL TOLERANCE

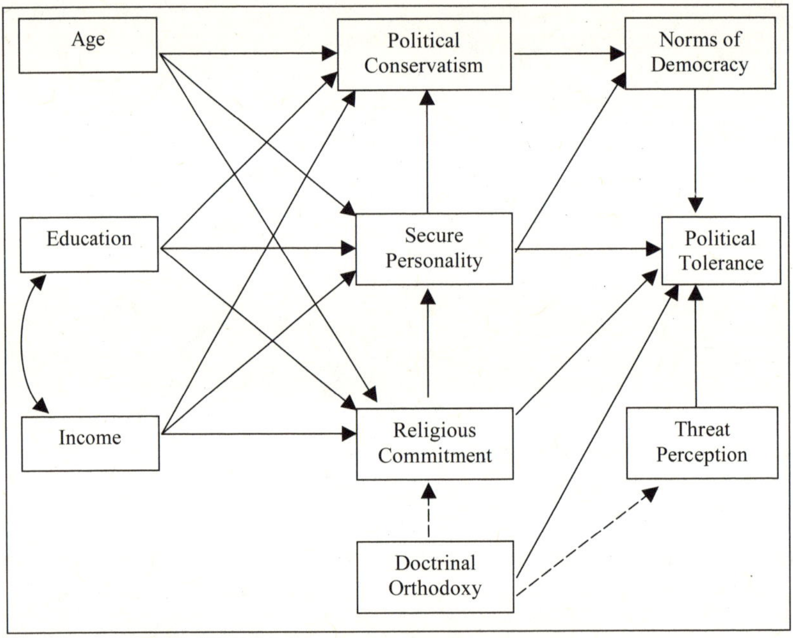

Results for Advanced Model

My first hypothesis—that increased religious commitment will lead to increased political intolerance—cannot be supported. Instead of increased religious commitment leading to decreased tolerance, the model shows a nominal increase in political tolerance with a path coefficient of .12 ($p < .04$). This is an extremely noteworthy finding, particularly when increased doctrinal orthodoxy has such a strong influence on religious commitment (.43). Surely, if religious commitment does not negatively influence political tolerance when so great an impact is made by high levels of doctrinal orthodoxy, then religious commitment can be said to truly have an influence contrary to the results of scores of earlier studies. Likewise, the second hypothesis does not obtain support (increased doctrinal orthodoxy leads to increased intolerance) because the path coefficient is inconsequential and not significant. This finding is extraordinary because doctrinal orthodoxy (e.g., fundamentalism) is promoted routinely as directly contributing to political intolerance in American society. Yet, the evidence here cannot support such a position.

Figure 2.5

Results for Advanced Model of Political Tolerance

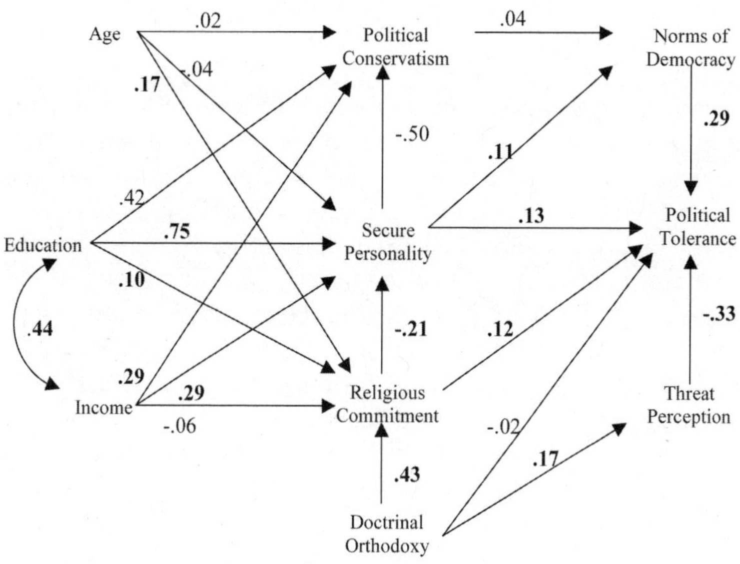

Thus, my third hypothesis—that the unmediated or direct relationship between religious commitment and doctrinal orthodoxy demonstrated in past research is spurious—is supported. But, that support comes with an important caveat. There is no direct negative effect that either religious commitment or doctrinal orthodoxy has on political tolerance, but the results do show that for both variables, an indirect negative effect on political tolerance exists. This is the result of the influence of doctrinal orthodoxy on threat perception, the influence of doctrinal orthodoxy on religious commitment, and the influence of religious commitment on a secure personality.

These relationships demonstrate that religion has an indirect influence on political tolerance so that increased religious commitment and increased doctrinal orthodoxy lead to increased intolerance via other variables. In terms of doctrinal orthodoxy, increased doctrinal orthodoxy leads to increased levels of threat perception, which is consistent with the research of Wilcox and Jelen (1990). This is an important finding because increased threat perception leads to decreased political tolerance (-.33 $p < .001$). Part of the significance of this finding is that it leads one to question what it is about high levels of doctrinal orthodoxy (in contrast to lower levels of doctrinal orthodoxy) that leads to increased levels of threat perception (a question that the current data cannot answer). Another large component of the significance of this finding is, as Gibson (2006) has so lucidly outlined, research has yet to explain the variance in the threat perception variable, while demonstrating that (seemingly) logical connections, such as personality attributes influencing threat perception, cannot be maintained (Gibson 2006, 24). Where doctrinal orthodoxy will fit into future research on explaining the variance in threat perception is not known at this time, particularly since future research on understanding the variation in threat perception has so many potential avenues of research (Gibson 2006, 24–25).

The relationship between religious belief and religious behavior (Leege & Kellstedt 1993; Layman & Green 1998) also garners robust support as increased levels of doctrinal orthodoxy (belief) lead to increased religious commitment (behavior); the parameter estimate is a substantial .43 ($p < .001$). In turn, increased religious commitment does lead to a decrease in a secure personality. This is important because one of the two components of a secure personality is dogmatism (e.g., open versus closed mind; the other component is self-esteem). Therefore, as religious commitment increases, an individual is more likely to have a closed mind and decreased levels of self-esteem. The total indirect effect of religious commitment on political tolerance is -.034, and the total indirect effect of doctrinal orthodoxy on political tolerance is -.10. The finding that is different than what we might expect is the influence of education on religious commitment. The path coefficient is a weak one (.10), but it is statistically significant and is in the opposite direction than anticipated.

An attempt is not being made to reassess the predictors of political tolerance that are well established in the literature, but some of the other path coefficients are worth a mention. Both of the political predictors of political tolerance—threat perception and support for norms of democracy—demonstrate consistency with past research (Sullivan et al. 1982; Marcus et al. 1995). Increased support for norms of democracy leads to an increase in political tolerance, while increased levels of threat perception lead to a decrease in political tolerance. The influence of a secure personality on political tolerance also performs as expected as does its influence on support for norms of democracy (Sullivan et al. 1982).

The path coefficient from political conservatism to norms of democracy is much different than the results obtained by Sullivan, Piereson, and Marcus, who reported a statistically significant path coefficient of -.41 for this relationship. The difference in results may be because Sullivan and the other authors measured political conservatism with two indicators, not one, as was done here. They also were able to measure support for norms of democracy with seven items instead of two, which may account for the differences in the results.[10] A similar explanation is likely to have influenced the results for the paths from a secure personality to support for norms of democracy and from a secure personality to political tolerance. In both instances, the path coefficient is smaller than expected (.11 and .13, respectively). Sullivan et al. (1982) used four separate cumulative scales as observed variables to measure a secure personality: dogmatism, self-esteem, faith in people, and value-actualization (a scale based on Maslow's hierarchy). The last two constructs had the weakest impact and were excluded from this analysis.

Religious Traditions

The results so far focused on a religious model of political tolerance without distinction between the various religious traditions. Another analysis of the same advanced model presented in figure 2.4, however, present results for each religious tradition. As with the presentation of religious tradition earlier in the chapter, I analyzed each tradition separately (as opposed to using dummy variables). Remember, this advanced model can only assess three religious traditions—evangelical protestants, mainline protestants, and Catholics—because individuals classified as secular were not asked the doctrinal orthodoxy question.

In figure 2.6, the path coefficients are shown. All coefficients are the standardized estimates and all coefficients in bold print indicate significance at .05 or better. To delineate the estimates for each tradition, C is for Catholic, M is for mainline protestant, and E is for evangelical protestant. The sample size for Catholics is 219, evangelical protestants 120, and mainline protestants 99. I present figure 2.6 in two parts. Part A depicts the results for all the variables in the model with the exception of the demographic variables (age, education, and income). In Part B, the results for age, education, and income are depicted. The results are represented in two parts to simplify the presentation of the data and to make it easier to read and understand. However, the model was estimated, as figure 2.4 depicts, as a single structural equation model in which all parameter estimates were obtained at once, not in two different stages.

Figure 2.6A

Advanced Model Results by Religious Tradition

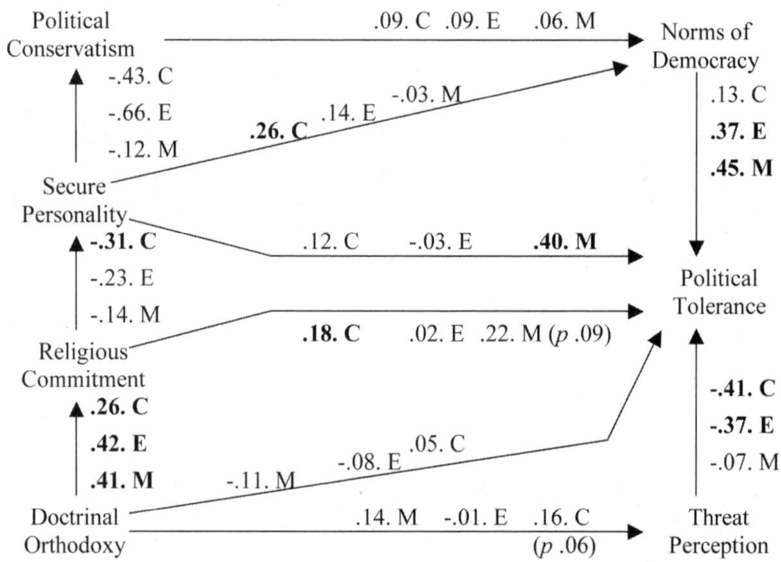

A quick look at figure 2.6A shows that, once again, there is no support for the first hypothesis, which is that increased religious commitment will lead to increased political intolerance. For the evangelical protestant tradition, the relationship is nonexistent; for Catholics, increased religious commitment leads to more—not less—political tolerance; even the mainline protestant result is counter to the hypothesis with increased commitment leading to increased tolerance. Although this path coefficient is not statistically significant at .05 or less, with a *p* value of .09, this should be given consideration because the mainline protestant model has the smallest sample size of 99 respondents. Likewise, there is no support for the second hypothesis, which is that doctrinal orthodoxy has a direct effect on political tolerance whereby increased orthodoxy leads to increased intolerance. None of the path coefficients for the three religious traditions obtained statistical significance. Therefore, similar to the results for all respondents (collectively), my third hypothesis for each religious tradition is supported.

For the other relationships of interest, the results are mixed. For the influence of doctrinal orthodoxy on threat perception, the Catholic tradition demonstrates increased orthodoxy leading to increased threat perception (*p* .06). The Mainline tradition is in the predicted direction, but it is not a significant parameter estimate, and the evangelical tradition shows an inconsequential relationship (substantively and statistically). Nevertheless, doctrinal orthodoxy leads to increased religious commitment for all three religious traditions and, increased religious commitment does lead to a less secure personality for all three religious traditions, although only the parameter estimate for Catholics is statistically significant. An important question (although it is outside the focus of the present analysis) is why religious commitment may lead to more dogmatism/less self-esteem (e.g., a decreased secure personality) for Catholics in contrast to mainline or evangelical protestants.

In reviewing figure 2.6B, one interesting finding is the relationship between education and religious commitment. This relationship was contrary to expectations for the model shown in figure 2.5 without distinction between religious traditions. This finding holds when assessing the traditions separately. Increased education leads to increased religious commitment for evangelical protestants and mainline protestants (the *p* value of .10 for mainline protestants is arguably significant given its smaller sample of 99). This finding might be perceived as more explicable for the mainline protestant tradition, but for the evangelical tradition, there is typically an anti-intellectual bias that this finding challenges.

Figure 2.6B

MODEL RESULTS BY RELIGIOUS TRADITION

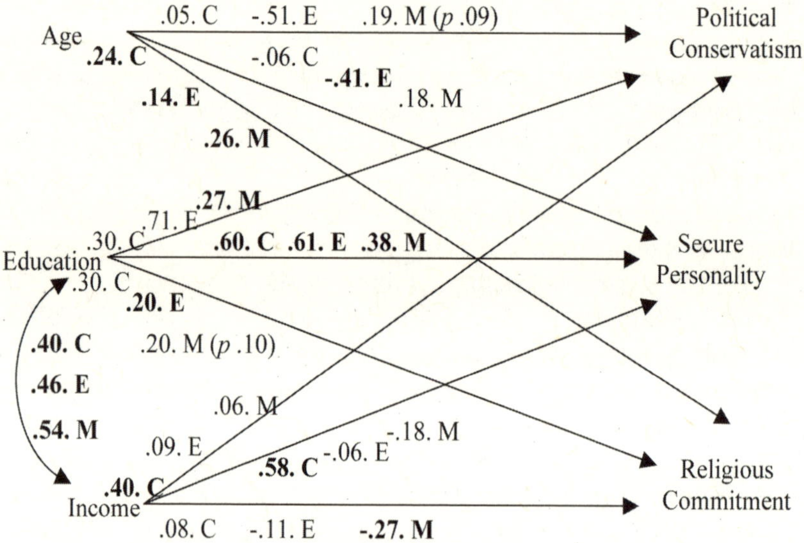

Discussion

The specific purpose of this chapter has been to reexamine the link between religion and political tolerance in a comprehensive analysis employing a sophisticated structural model with the pertinent psychological and political predictors of political tolerance; a "least-liked" measure of political tolerance; and religion variables representing belief, belonging, and behavior. This reexamination yielded results contrary to expectations. First, increased religious commitment did not directly lead to decreased levels of political tolerance and doctrinal orthodoxy did not directly lead to decreased political tolerance. Thus, my third hypothesis—that the direct relationship between both religious commitment and doctrinal orthodoxy (demonstrated in past research) to political tolerance is spurious—was supported but with an important caveat. That caveat was that religious commitment and doctrinal orthodoxy contributed to an indirect negative influence on political tolerance, particularly when there was no distinction made between religious traditions. Finally, the influence of education on religious commitment was contrary to expectations; increased education resulted in more—not less—religious commitment.

This is the first research to use the Sullivan et al. (1982) "least-liked" tolerance measure when examining the relationship between religious commitment and political tolerance, and this may be what accounts for the different results obtained here in which increased religious commitment leads to increased and not decreased political tolerance. The least-liked measurement approach is meant to control for the ideological bias of the GSS items, which are the most frequently used political tolerance items. It is meant also to disentangle attitudes toward a group versus the actions taken by a group. By using the least-liked measurement approach to tolerance, Sullivan et al. (1982) was able to diminish the differences in political tolerance across the various religious traditions.

Although their study did not present results in terms of how religious commitment related to their least-liked political tolerance measures, their logic on tolerance appropriately can be extended to the relationship between religious commitment and political tolerance. Most research that focuses on religion inevitably distinguishes between religious individuals with differing levels of religious commitment, noting increased commitment relating to increased intolerance. It makes sense that in the same way Sullivan et al. (1982) saw the relationship between religious tradition and political tolerance change, here the direct relationship between religious commitment and political tolerance has changed.

In addition, the results presented here are also a consequence of the inclusion of important political and psychological predictors of political tolerance. That is, now that these variables are included in a religious model of political tolerance, the direct negative relationship typically found between religion and political tolerance does not manifest. Beyond that, the reason for the divergence of the current results from previous studies on political tolerance, I argue, is attributed to the natural political maturation of different religious sectors, the changing demographics of the religious community,[11] and the acceptance of democratic norms within the contemporary American Christian community (all of which was discussed in chapter 1).

Although it may seem axiomatic within the discipline of political science that religion is incompatible with political tolerance, the results shown here for the direct influence of religious commitment and doctrinal orthodoxy on political tolerance tell a different story. The story it tells is that religion is not inherently incompatible with liberal democratic values. I have completed the first complex step in demonstrating my simple contention that we have, as a liberal democratic society in the United States, nothing to fear from the religiously inclined among us. Their religious behavior does not incline them toward intolerance; neither are they less (or more) tolerant than their secular counterparts.

The focus of the next chapter is on a qualitative assessment of the link between religion and political tolerance. Focus groups are used so that, in contrast to the preceding empirical analysis, religious individuals are enabled to speak to us, in their own words, as to how they navigate the relationship between faith and liberal democracy.

Chapter 3

What Do Christian Congregants Say about Themselves?

In sepulchral black and red, the cover of Time magazine dated April 8, 1966—Good Friday—introduced millions of readers to existential anguish with the question "Is God Dead?" If he was, the likely culprit was science. . . . Nobody would write such an article now. . . . A major poll . . . reveals a breadth of tolerance and curiosity virtually across the religious spectrum.

—Newsweek *(August 29, 2005-September 5 issue), Jerry Adler*

The results from the previous chapter suggest that increased religious commitment does not directly lead to decreased levels of political tolerance and higher levels of doctrinal orthodoxy do not directly lead to decreased political tolerance. Also, increased education corresponded with more, rather than less, religious commitment, and the results suggested that the relationship between religious commitment and doctrinal orthodoxy with political tolerance indeed may be spurious. Nevertheless, popular conception, particularly within academic circles, would offer a different portrait regarding individuals of religious faith in America. What that vision would look like, in all likelihood, is what Rodney Stark (2001, 254) in *One True God: Historical Consequences of Monotheism* describes—true religious believers "are stupid, crazy, ignorant, and dangerous." In fact, recent scholarship has begun to examine the attitudes of educational elites toward Christian conservatives. Bolce and De Maio (1999a) demonstrated that there is an extreme level of antagonism and antipathy against Christian conservatives, particularly among the highly educated and secular, and they suggest this may have implications for political tolerance.

> The historic negative relationship between educational attainment and prejudice is reversed with regard to feelings toward Christian fundamentalists. At present, a significant plurality (37 percent) of highly educated non-fundamentalists hold intensely antagonistic feelings toward Christian fundamentalists, and another 19 percent view members of this religious group unfavorably. These data do no permit us to determine whether this antipathy stems from attempts to guard democratic civility and pluralism, or instead from cultural and religious bias. . . . Justified or not, it is antipathy all the same. . . . Social scientists, however, might want to reconsider the implications for American pluralism and theories of prejudice when the most extreme manifestations of antipathy toward religious out-groups are more likely to be found among the highly educated than among the less educated classes. (Bolce & De Maio 1999a, 55)[1]

Moreover, it has been suggested that the religious right is considered a "reference group" to which individuals associate certain attitudes and behaviors (Bolce & De Maio 1999b). Bolce and De Maio (1999b, 509–10) assert that "[f]rom the perspective of some in the media, Christian fundamentalists are the Christian Right, a political movement whose views on abortion, school prayer, and homosexuality they perceive as intolerant, extreme, and antipluralistic. . . ." That is, the conservative issue-attitude position of many conservative Christians associated with the religious right is considered by the elite media to be prima facie evidence of intolerance.

Because of these conflicting portraits of religious individuals, it is important to hear what individuals of faith have to say about the relationship between faith and democracy, in their own words.[2] There is no lack of empirical objective analyses about religion and religious individuals in our country, rarely have those under study—religious individuals themselves—been interviewed so that their subjective viewpoints on liberal democracy and their participation in it, as well as their views and definition regarding political tolerance can be ascertained. Therefore, in this chapter, I turn to a qualitative assessment (specifically, focus group analysis) of the linkage between Christian congregants and their understanding of the relationship between their faith and their role as citizens in a liberal democracy. As such, this chapter presents a necessary (subjective) contextual substance, sorely lacking within the discipline of political science, to the empirical foundation, allowing for a more complex understanding of our topic. Although a portion of this discussion includes an explicit discussion about religion and political tolerance, it goes beyond that particular topic. The primary purpose of this chapter is to explore how religious individuals themselves navigate the relationship between their faith and participation in a liberal democracy in general, which includes political tolerance. Doing so allows us to assess the theoretical argument of Kraynak (2001) that Christians in the contemporary United States view liberal democracy as the preferred (even God-ordained) system of governance (discussed in chapter 1). Given Kraynak's arguments, we should expect to see such sentiments expressed during the focus group sessions.

Focus Groups as a Research Strategy

A focus group is a planned discussion or conversation (Krueger & Casey 2000). It can also be defined as a group interview with a focus on "interaction within the group" and not a mere exchange between participants and moderator (Morgan 1998, 9). Focus group sessions are typically recorded on audiotape and (often) videotaped. The primary advantage of using focus groups in research is that it allows for a particular topic to be discussed and explored, in an in-depth fashion, with participants using their own words (Morgan 1988; Krueger & Casey 2000; Stewart, Shamdasani, & Rook 2007). Because the focus group conversation is not closely or tightly controlled, participants are allowed to respond in an interactive format and express a range of opinions and views (Morgan 1988; Krueger & Casey 2000; Stewart et al. 2007), and this group interaction allows for more and better information to emerge than from a series of single interviews (Krueger & Casey 2000; Stewart et al. 2007). An interactive group format allowing for a broad expression of views is particularly useful (and important) when the topic involves religion or an individual's religious faith because the way in which individuals perceive the relationship between their faith or religion and their role in society is wrought with nuance and complexity.

To be sure, focus group research also has its drawbacks. These drawbacks have hampered the acceptance of such research in the social sciences in general. The area of inquiry that has used focus group research most often over the last five decades is marketing research, although social scientists Merton, Fiske, and Kendall (1956) first introduced the techniques (Krueger & Casey 2000). Although this technique is beginning to appear in scholarly political science journals and manuscripts (including Conover, Crewe, and Searing [1991] and Hibbing and Theiss-Morse [1995]), it is still rarely used. The problems with the technique are important to note. There is, for example, no ability to generalize from the focus group to a larger population; that is, the results from one focus group cannot be claimed as representative of any particular group or other population (Stewart et al. 2007; Conover et al. 1991) because participants are not obtained in a random fashion. The ability to replicate focus group research is also very difficult. No matter how well structured a format, there is simply no way to re-create precisely the dynamics of a single focus group session in another session. Thus, while an advantage of using focus groups is that it allows for open-ended responses and a free-flowing conversation to reveal what participants are thinking and what they believe about a topic, the inherent disadvantage regarding replication remains.

In addition, although some information coming out of focus groups is often not possible in individual interviews, individual responses are not independent of the responses of others in the group. Furthermore, the potential exists for opinionated members of the focus group to dominate the discussion, resulting in more reserved focus group members participating less; and this has the potential to bias any results (Stewart et al. 2007). Similarly, moderator bias can play a role, which occurs when focus group participants provide responses that they believe the moderator wants to hear. In fact, in a critique of focus group research done by the Kettering Foundation, Nelson Polsby (1993, 84) found that "A really skilled moderator ought to be able in two short hours to get a focus group of 'approximately 12 people' to say nearly anything."

Even so, the drawbacks are outweighed by the benefits. If we are going to begin to understand how individuals of faith perceive liberal democracy and their role in it, we are going to need to hear what these individuals have to say themselves—in a format that allows for open-ended conversation—and we must listen to how these individuals talk about issues and the language they use. Although generalizability with focus group results is extremely limited, focus groups can provide insights and a depth of information not possible with surveys in which generalizing is possible. In responding to Polsby's critique, Michael Briand (1993, 542) argued that focus groups allow us "to get at the concerns, needs, and feelings that underlie people's opinions and preferences." He went on to state that "Even the best scholarly surveys only aggregate opinion—they merely sum individual views. . . . There just is no genuinely public view until the individual members of the public have thought and talked together about what they, as a public, believe, feel, and want" (Briand 1993, 543). Furthermore, the drawbacks of focus group research can be minimized. The focus group results presented here, of necessity, will be grounded and judged by the empirical data presented in chapter 2, so coupling the qualitative focus group data with the empirical survey data minimizes the drawbacks (Hibbing & Theiss-Morse 1995 made just such an argument); the weaknesses in survey research are minimized as well (addressing the comments by Polsby and Briand).

Framework and Method of Analysis

The analysis that follows is based on four focus group sessions conducted in Lake County, Indiana. Each focus group consisted of 10 to 14 individuals (men and women) who were a minimum of 18 years of age. In addition, each focus group session was comprised of congregants from different churches located in Lake County.[3] Four separate religious traditions were represented: a black protestant church, an evangelical protestant church, a mainline protestant church, and a Catholic church; three of the four religious traditions are consistent with the religious traditions analyzed in chapter 2.[4] In this way, the assessments presented in this chapter can be used to illuminate the previous empirical work. Another important factor in using religious tradition as a means of constructing the four focus groups is the issue of homogeneity or compatibility. It is important that there be sufficient homogeneity among focus group participants to allow for an environment in which participants are willing to openly express their views and opinions (Krueger & Casey 2000; Stewart et al. 2007). In short, the participants of each focus group must have something in common to help create a "comfortable, permissive environment" (Krueger & Casey 2000, 9).

Each focus group was comprised of members from the same religious institution, and religious tradition is one of two key components the participants had in common. The other key component was that participants attended their particular religious institution at least once a week. They had similar levels of religious commitment, or put differently, they each had a minimum level of religious commitment. Because discussing religion or faith is a sensitive topic, using religious tradition and a minimum standard of religious commitment as the key aspects of commonality for the focus group participants of each focus group session helped create a "comfortable and permissive" environment.[5]

Each focus group was asked the same questions. Appendix B contains a complete copy of the focus group script that was used in each session. The moderator was asked to use what Hibbing and Theiss-Morse (1995, 87) called a "minimalist strategy, trying to keep the herd in the pasture but providing as little other guidance as possible." Not only does this minimize any potential moderator bias, but it gets to the heart of the intent of these focus groups. Given the lack of focus group research within political science, in general (and at the intersection of religion and politics, in particular), casting as broad a net as possible would allow respondents to express their beliefs and views based on their own particular perspectives. To that end, I worked to provide as little structure as possible so that no particular worldview was imposed on the participants.

While the focus groups were conducted and moderated by Survey Research Services (a professional research services firm), I watched the sessions from a separate room via a live television feed with real-time viewing capability. By having a professional focus group moderator[6] and by viewing the session as it was happening (and not being in the room during it), I accomplished several goals. First, my absence minimized bias regarding respondents' answers. In addition, the company and the moderator conducting the sessions were from outside the community and the moderator was someone who had no connection to the local religious community. Thus, the potential for moderator bias was minimized. Second, the real-time viewing capability allowed me to take notes and send information to the moderator when necessary. Finally, this setup facilitated the videotaping and voice recording of all four focus group sessions for later reference.

The focus groups were held in the evening on April 24 and 25, 2006. Each focus group lasted approximately ninety minutes, and two focus group sessions were held each night. On April 24, the black protestant congregation focus group session began at 5:00 p.m. and ended at approximately 6:30 p.m. The second focus group session, with an evangelical protestant congregation, began at 7:00 p.m. and ended promptly at 8:30 p.m. On April 25, from 5:00 p.m. through 6:30 p.m., the focus group session with the Catholic congregation occurred. Finally, at 7:00 p.m. to 8:30 p.m., the final focus group session was conducted (with a mainline protestant congregation). Table 3.1 lists essential information about the sessions, including the religious affiliations, dates of sessions, and number of participants in each focus group session.

Table 3.1
FOCUS GROUP SESSION INFORMATION

Religious Tradition	*Date*	*Length of Session*	*Time Started*	*Number of Participants*
Black Protestant	April 24, 2006	90 minutes	5:00 p.m.	13
Evangelical Protestant	April 24, 2006	90 minutes	7:00 p.m.	12
Catholic	April 25, 2006	90 minutes	5:00 p.m.	10
Mainline Protestant	April 25, 2006	90 minutes	7:00 p.m.	14

The congregations were chosen in a nonrandom fashion. I compiled a list of congregations that had been provided to me by contacts at a local church and a local Jewish federation office, both of which are in Munster, Indiana, a city located in Lake County, Indiana. I asked the local church and the federation office to provide me with a list of local religious institutions with whom they interacted. Furthermore, I requested of both groups that I be allowed to use their names in introducing myself. Thus, as I went about the process of acquiring the four congregations for participation in the focus groups, I called the senior leaders, introduced myself, and indicated that I had received their name from either the local church contact or the federation contact (whichever one was applicable). From that list, I contacted the senior religious leader of various congregations to request that I be allowed to recruit participants for the focus group study from their congregation membership. Once I received approval from the appropriate leader at each congregation, I provided fliers for distribution at each church (Appendix C contains a copy of the flier). Fliers were posted in prominent places at each congregation and (when possible) placed in the weekly bulletin that was handed out during Sunday services.[7] Participation was determined on a "first come" basis, meaning that the individuals selected were the first ones who responded to the request for participation. When I received a call from a potential participant, I took down their name and congregational affiliation. I then screened them for level of religious commitment by asking them if they attended services at least once a week and I also screened them for age by inquiring whether they were 18 years of age or older (Appendix D contains a copy of the phone transcript). Each focus group participant was paid $30.00 cash at the completion of the session.

The analysis of each focus group session is transcript-based; each focus group produced between 24 to 26 pages of transcribed text.[8] The transcripts were analyzed in several (iterative) steps. First, the transcripts were read through to reinforce the scope and purpose of the focus groups as well as to refresh my memory of what was said and in what context. Second, categories were created, based on the questions asked of the focus group participants. Each focus group transcript was then reread, and each statement was coded according to the classification scheme. If statements made in response to questions related to one category actually fit into a different category, then the statement was placed into that different category. Participant responses, not the researchers' questions, were the dominant drivers in determining where a statement was appropriately categorized. When statements did not fit into any of the original categories, those statements were reread and, when necessary, a new or different category was created. Once all the transcripts were analyzed and categorized in this manner, the statements compiled into each category were then reread to ensure that each separate participant statement was categorized accurately. This process is based upon the analysis strategy as outlined in Krueger and Casey (2000, chap. 6),

In Their Own Words

The following analysis revolves around the important themes of faith and citizenship, faith-based issues, political tolerance, and the relationship between church and state. These are the categories into which focus group participant responses were sorted. Because of the importance of religious tradition in religion and politics research, within each of these themes, I first present the results of each religious tradition. Once that is done, I provide an analysis and discussion of those results.

Faith and Citizenship

After a preliminary introduction and being asked about their general behavior as citizens, the participants were asked specifically about the influence of their faith on how they act as citizens. Although the specific question focused on their behavior as citizens (see Appendix B), it is clear that the participants in all four focus groups perceived the question to be about what motivates their civic or political participation (or lack thereof).

Black Protestant

The influence of race at the intersection of faith and citizenship was extensive in both depth and breadth. In fact, the influence of race on every aspect of the discussion was very palpable for these participants. It was clear that for many of these participants, family (parents and grandparents), religion, church, and faith—intertwined with race—had been an ever-present part of their upbringing. An elderly woman, in her nineties, made exactly this point in some of her comments. She stated that she "grew up on the brinks of slavery" in the South. "My parents taught us that we should live by faith and she [my mother] always said that there will be a better day." However, this was not a blind faith but one coupled with action; that is, the participants expressed that faith had to be coupled with something tangible. The same elderly woman who spoke of learning from her parents to have faith in a better tomorrow went on to say, "So you get on your knees and pray for the Lord to send you a job, but you don't get up the next morning and drink coffee and sit down. Faith is an action word."

In similar fashion, the influence of faith on civic and political behavior for many participants came from the notion of having "dual" citizenship (citizenship here on earth as well as citizenship in the future kingdom of God). Thus, this "dual" citizenship had a very tangible place in reminding them that their behavior is known to God. As one participant put it, "I'm moving through life, if you will, to my eternal destination, [I] try to live as though I'm actually before God. He's a part of everything I do so when I'm tempted to run a red light, I remember, well first and foremost, it wouldn't honor

God." For some, the influence of faith meant developing the attitude to do the best they could in the service of others. For example, one individual stated:

> The way that my faith influences me and I think that over the course of my life has influenced me is to develop myself [so] that I can give the best possible service to others. And what I mean by that is, when I study the Bible and I see that Jesus was an activist in his community and he always worked to not only continually learn about people, but also educate people in a better way. Individually, what I have tried to do is get the best possible education [for] myself, [because] it means the education could be a benefit to others.

There was also an extensive amount of feedback as to the importance of community in terms of civic participation. The wider community was considered extremely important, to the point of it being considered one's extended family, and there was a clear need to ensure that the community was maintained successfully, and therefore, was of pivotal importance. One participant stated that sentiment by saying, "You know, as far as citizenship is concerned, looking at everyone as my family."

Evangelical Protestant

In this group of evangelical protestants, godly behavior was mentioned most often as the motivation for the influence of faith on citizenship. These evangelical protestants were likely to state that belief in God motivates them to behave right, which means that they should obey the laws of the land. One woman said that "God is the one that motivated me to live right and to obey the laws." In part, this motivation was driven by an acknowledgment that institutions are put here by God. As another participant stated, "I try to conform to being the citizen that I think you should be just because God put those things on earth, those organizations." So being a good citizen or participating in civic society was motivated not just because it was the right thing to do, in general, but it was motivated by the knowledge that order is ultimately established by God. As yet another individual said, "I don't want to get a ticket, I don't want to not pay my taxes and . . . have the IRS come after me. . . . Ultimately it all comes from God, there is a thing in our hearts, that I don't want to get in trouble, and I don't want to dishonor God either."

Also expressed was the sentiment that one needs to be involved in community so as to ensure that future generations are left with a "better place" to live. Typically, this was expressed in terms of responsibility; there was a responsibility to God and future generations to keep society as free from evil and immorality as possible. The participants in this focus group had many examples of "putting feet" to their prayers and intentions. One participant told of a salon where she gets her nails done every week; she further mentioned that she very much liked where she has her nails done and would tell others about the business and her particular manicurist. On one visit some sexually explicit and "lewd" shows were televised and she made a point to go to the owner of the salon and let her know that such programming was problematic and that she would no longer recommend that business to others if this is the type of programming that would be showed, especially since children are routinely in the salon with their mothers. This is just one such story told by participants in this focus group. These individuals expressed a very real sense that they were to participate in civic society, that doing so was something that God wanted them to do, and that they must be willing to put their faith into action. As one individual put it, they were interested in "putting feet" on their prayers and their faith. Another individual said "I don't know how we can open up the Book that we are suppose to base our faith on and not see where we are commanded to speak up, to be part of, to stand for the rights of the person. How can you not see that we are to be involved?"

A different individual indicated a belief that "we are called by God to be salt and light to the world and we are to be basically the moral compass for our country, and if we don't stand up and voice our opinion how can we [be that moral compass]." Another said, "I think having prayer and calling for the church to pray for the nation is great. But after prayer, you have to get up and do something." It was very apparent, as evidenced by the number of different stories shared about specific incidents and events, that individuals in this focus group placed a premium on a real and tangible connection between their faith and the verbal expression of their faith (e.g., what they say) and the actions they took as everyday citizens in their communities. These participants expressed a general belief that to not be part of ones' (larger) civic community by making your voice heard was to "fall short" of what they should be doing. This coincided with the argument that one had a responsibility for oneself, one's community, and future generations and that individuals needed to try to meet those responsibilities (e.g., to not "fall short"). One participant nicely summed up the sentiment by stating, "We need to be out there as much as possible and take responsibility for ourselves and our country and I think when we do we won't blame other people."

Catholic

When asked about how faith influences their behavior as citizens, such as political and/or civic participation, the Catholic focus group participants had, in terms of quantity, less to say about this topic than the other three focus groups and respective religious traditions. There was an emphasis on the early influences relating to civic participation and the role of faith; those early influences were first and foremost instilled at a very young age by family (parents and grandparents), as well as by nuns and priests in grade school and lay church leaders in high school. There was a general discussion about rights coupled with responsibility, and the responsibility was both to one's community (here on earth) as well as to the future kingdom of God (as a Christian). There was, however, special emphasis placed on standing up in the face of injustice and for more education from the church so that, in the words of one participant, "we can continue to grow and learn from each other, and fully base our political decisions on what we have as [a] faith." In fact, one participant emphatically stated that "I think it's the church's job to educate us in the true Christian meaning, [even though] we still have to make our own decisions by our own consciences." Thus, the general tone was that the church needed to provide the education in Christian and church beliefs so that one had the tools necessary for political decision-making, but as a Christian, ultimately, how one chooses to use what he or she knows is entirely within the purview of the individual.

Mainline Protestant

The most pervasive and dominant theme for these focus group participants regarding the discussion of faith and citizenship was the interconnection between faith and behavior and the foundation of faith as the basis for all behavior, whether civic, political, or otherwise. More so than the other three focus groups, individuals in this focus group explicitly mentioned the foundation of faith as the cornerstone for all other behavior. For these participants, the influence of faith was ever present and ever real. For several in the group, faith was cited as a major influence on how they voted and chose their elected officials. When speaking of faith and citizenship, one participant said "But there is no question for a Christian, you can't separate the two [faith and citizenship] because it's a part of your whole life, it's how you view things." More than once someone in the group made the point that "Your faith and civic duty and those things, your relationship to your fellow man is all intertwined."

The second theme mentioned by several individuals in this focus group session was the importance of personal responsibility. For them, the church and faith gave one a sense of having a personal responsibility that included good citizenship. Furthermore, part of good citizenship was to be involved in helping others. One individual even indicated that in participating and attempting to do good (civic) works, the principle of love that the Bible teaches means that there is a need to assess "who is it hurting, who is it helping, [and] is it serving the kind of love that Christ lived for." What was very clear from these participants is that their faith and Christianity provided them with a worldview and that this worldview influenced everything they did.

Faith-based Issues

Each focus group session was also asked about faith-based issues. They were prompted to identify faith-based issues and were specifically asked how faith influences their involvement or opinions on those issues. In addition, each focus group was asked whether their faith, in terms of faith-based issues, caused them any type of conflict. Thus, each group was able to discuss and identify those faith-based issues that resonated with them, as opposed to being asked specific questions about issues such as abortion or euthanasia. As with the previous section, I will discuss the results from each focus group separately.

Black Protestant

In contrast to the other focus groups, the black protestant focus group participants did not focus on faith-based issues in quite the same way as the others. For one, they said far less (in quantity only) than any of the other focus groups, specifically, about what traditionally are considered faith-based issues. Secondly, a consistent theme ran through their entire focus group session and it was present when asked about faith-based issues. In particular, an emphasis was placed on their influences as children, including that of faith and the church as they pertained to faith-based issues in contemporary America. The general discussion revolved around how, today, those childhood foundational influences have deteriorated. One participant stated, "It goes back to the parents, what you allow to happen in your home, you can't stand there and tell me that you didn't know your child was watching this on TV or you don't know your child was playing video games."

These focus group participants identified faith-based issues when asked (they brought up pro-life, pro-choice, cloning, and same sex marriage), but they did not focus on these issues in terms of which side of the issue they were on. Rather, they focused on them in terms of how the issues lined up with what the Bible told them and whether or not those faith-based issues were being properly enforced in the children—giving the children a good foundation of morals—rather than on trying to legislate what others have the right to do or not to do. There was also a concern raised that television and other media outlets were inundating children with less-than-positive images and that there was not adequate legislation to protect the children from influences that children should be sheltered from at young ages. To sum up, there was an intertwined concern relating to faith-based issues: the breakdown of the family, which hurts the foundational underpinnings provided to the next generation, intertwined with a pervasive media influence that exposes young children to negative influences.

Evangelical Protestant

This focus group did not discuss faith-based issues in the sense of whether or not they directly agreed or disagreed with certain policies. Rather, much of their discussion regarding identifiable contemporary faith-based issues had to do with inappropriate material, such as a television show viewed at a salon or a pornographic magazine that was in clear view at a local gas station. And the issue for these individuals was not centered on whether or not those shows or magazines had a right to be shown or sold, but rather it focused on airing or selling such material where children can be influenced. It also had to do with their sense of personal morality. Two participants indicated that they did not want to spend their money at a business that would promote adult material, particularly when it is done in a manner demonstrating disregard for who might be subjected to such material. The issue, for these participants, went beyond agreement or disagreement (e.g., they were not advocating prohibiting the production and distribution of sexually illicit material) and went to putting their faith into action. This is very much the same motivational theme that permeated their motivations for civic behavior and political involvement. For this group, putting faith and tangible action together—whether or not it relates to strictly civic and/or political issues such as voting or to faith-based issues such as the promotion of sexually explicit material—is important for these participants. One very poignant and telling theme came from a young woman of college age. In thinking about faith-based issues and the involvement of her faith community, she had this to say:

> I would have to say that we should be more involved. We can always be more involved. The one thing that I have a problem with . . . in the church as a whole, I think, as Christians, we need to focus more on preaching compassion and love instead of condemnation and judgment. There is right and wrong. God is very plain in the Bible, it's black and white as far as I am concerned. But I think that a lot of times in the public eyes and what you see on television, what you hear on radio, you [are] always hearing the bad side of the church. God hates this, God hates that. And it's, like, our job as Christians is to be as much like Jesus as we can and Jesus did not go around condemning people, making people feel bad about their problems. He preached love, he preached compassion and he got down to people's level and I don't think that there is nearly enough of that in the church.

In response to this, another member of the focus group pointed out that Jesus did confront wrong doing and wrongdoers, but that he "did it in the right way." And another participant added, in agreement with the young woman, that "Christians are really good [at] talking about we need prayer in the public school, [but] . . . they don't pray at home or don't come to prayer meetings at church." This same individual went on to argue that the problem with many Christians who talk about the problem of removing the Ten Commandments from public places is that these same individuals are, in all likelihood, unable to actually recite the Ten Commandments.

The implication was very clear; Christians who want more morality in the public square (e.g., such as posting of the Ten Commandments in a public place) must actually live the lifestyle they advocate. This was yet another dimension of coupling faith with action for these participants; it is not enough to merely talk about the Christian life or Christian values but that life and those values must be lived. This is not to say that these participants did not recognize moral dilemmas presented by certain policies, such as abortion. In fact, they acknowledged that not everyone in society adheres to their particular Christian worldview and that this will create dilemmas in the public square. Nevertheless, their emphasis was mainly on them, as individuals and as a community of faith, striving to do better in living the life they felt called to live.

Catholic

Several faith-based issues were raised by the Catholic focus group participants, including abortion, illegal immigration, and social justice (in a general discussion). The abortion discussion was brief and pointed. One woman, who had a husband in local elected office, made the point that oftentimes candidates are asked whether or not they are pro-life (e.g., the official Catholic position), irrespective of whether or not the office they are running for has any influence or control over abortion policy. She said, "Many times though when we're asking that to the politician, he will not have the ability to use that in his job performance, if his job performance is strictly approving budgets . . . . And to vote against a person because they said, well I'm pro-life or I'm not pro-life, I think you really have to look at what the job also entails to say is that going to make a difference." No one criticized or openly disagreed with the Catholic Church's pro-life position; however, a few participants raised issues juxtaposing competing demands or issues with abortion (such as the earlier quote). One participant pointed out that society was always going to have abortion and that this individual was far more interested in the Catholic Church being involved with those losing their jobs. "But there's other issues that I think if the Catholic Church wants to get involved in, it's the people that are losing their jobs, mills closing, jobs being outsourced, but I don't hear [the Church] crying out for, to help these people." Finally, another individual argued that it didn't matter whether a Catholic said he or she was pro-life or pro-choice; either way, the person was going to be attacked for it.

More so than the typical hot-button faith-based issues such as abortion or homosexual marriage (which was not brought up at all in this focus group session), the topic of social justice was brought up quite a few times. Examples include concerns about senior citizens having to choose between food and medicine, the inability of some to afford medical care and being denied admittance to certain hospitals, and even urban sprawl. However, the issue that received the most attention, in terms of time spent talking about that particular topic as well as the number of individuals who contributed to the discussion on that particular topic, was the issue of illegal immigration. Whatever the particular Catholic Church position may be on the issue, and no one in the focus group discussed or mentioned the official Church position, the individuals in this focus group, while having great empathy for the plight of illegal immigrants, were nonetheless very concerned that illegal immigration as it pertains to Mexico was very much out of control and that it posed great problems for the United States. Further, there was widespread agreement among these participants that we could not just "throw the doors open."

The issue was largely one of equity. As one individual stated, "I had to wait eleven years to come to this country, I had to have a job and a sponsor to come to this country . . . let other people do the same." A participant even questioned the equity to other potential immigrants fleeing less desirable circumstances, such as Cuban refugees. "They [the government] say you didn't reach America, it's not land, it's the ocean. Why send them [Cubans] back and not the Mexicans? Shouldn't they have been welcomed too? I just think it's unfair." Still other participants pointed out that illegal immigrants should not get a "free pass" to citizenship when they are, technically, in violation of U.S. laws. There was even discussion of how illegal immigrants are in a position to be abused in the United States by unscrupulous employers, leaving the illegal immigrants without protection or recourse. Furthermore, there was a real recognition that the Church tries to help all individuals by providing food, shelter, and the like but that the problem of illegal immigration is so overwhelming that it is a drain on resources, not just from the standpoint of the Church providing assistance but from the standpoint of all community institutions, including hospitals and schools. One person summarized this way: "And so . . . it [illegal immigration] presents a problem, a social problem, all around."

Mainline Protestant

For these focus group participants, their discussion of faith-based issues had a significant element of what can only be described as "soul searching." There was a palpable sense of tension between their faith and how it influences their opinions and involvement regarding contemporary faith-based issues. This tension was captured by one gentlemen who said:

> I think faith has to stay the same but the levels of understanding change with every age. Scriptures would talk about going out and preaching the gospel to the ends of the earth, and obviously, there was a time when we thought the world was flat. Scientific understanding, stem cell research, and all of these things, we know more about [them and] what's involved certainly than we would have a hundred years ago. And keeping the same principles of faith but applying them as we know more about people and human life, and know more about the world we live in.

Another example of this tension and soul searching is highlighted in the following: "When we meet our maker as we perceive him, there's going to be some things we were wrong on. The best we can do is to work out our salvation with fear and trembling and realize that we are fallible and . . . what we believe to be right may not be 100 percent right because we don't see the whole picture." A very important example of this tension and soul searching is the issue of capital punishment. As one man said, "Governor Ryan, or former Governor Ryan of Illinois, by what he did, he, to me, he caused me more agony because he proved to me that the system is broke." Thus, the tension between supporting capital punishment and realizing that the system is "broke" caused a great deal of agony for at least one member of this focus group.

One insightful observation came from a gentleman who, as a naturalized citizen, indicated that he previously lived under a dictatorship before living in the United States, and he talked about faith-based issues from a more contemporary historical standpoint. He argued that Watergate changed the "relationship between the state and the masses." In essence, he suggested that when the mass public was given the chance to question even the president of the United States, then the questioning of other institutional and societal norms began. In his own words, "you could question anyone in every institution and the church became a part of that questioning . . . Before 1972, gay rights were not questioned, abortion was not an issue, none of these issues that are issues today."

Political Tolerance

One of the goals of these focus groups was to assess what members of the four religious traditions had to say about political tolerance. Specifically, I wanted to know what political tolerance meant to these Christian individuals and what their reflections were on the need for political tolerance in a liberal democracy. Some of the results were anticipated, but others clearly were not. For example, the literature in political science on political tolerance has a well-defined definition of political tolerance—political tolerance is a willingness to extend civil liberties to those with whom you disagree; and disagreement is central to assessing the level of political tolerance. However, this is not how political tolerance was interpreted by any of the four focus groups. Even when a definition of political tolerance was provided, the feedback regarding it clearly demonstrated that the participants were speaking of something other than political tolerance as defined by academicians in political science. That is not to say that the results of the focus groups did not provide interesting and useful feedback, because they did. It is only to highlight that what we, as scholars, want participants to discuss and how we want them to discuss a concept or topic oftentimes are entirely different. The disconnect between definitions also highlights the need for structuring a political tolerance discussion in a fashion better suited to eliciting responses so scholars can make assessments relating to it. A discussion of this issue is taken up later in this chapter.

Black Protestant

When these focus group participants were asked about political tolerance, they approached it from a very different standpoint than the other three focus groups in that their responses contrasted political parties—Democrat versus Republican. When asked by the focus group moderator "What is political tolerance?," one woman responded with "Can you put up with President Bush?" Another individual spoke about having to tolerate President Bush at Coretta Scott King's funeral because he [the president] had to be there. "He is the president of the United States, he better be there. So you can bear that knowing the work that she's done that he would be at that funeral . . . so you have to tolerate it." This was further explained as not having any problem with accepting differences, but that "the problem comes when there is only one difference. That's the problem, today's Republican party, either you are here [with the Republican party] or you are un-American." In contrast, one individual did talk about having social/moral viewpoints, such as on abortion or homosexual marriage, based on the Bible. In talking about how his coworkers react to him, this individual said, "They don't want to talk about the Bible and biblical belief . . . but they want to force their beliefs on everyone else. . . . And when you say something like 'I don't believe in that, I don't believe in same sex marriage,' then you are labeled as not being tolerant."

Evangelical Protestant

In this focus group, participants generally spoke of political tolerance in terms of agreement; that is, whether or not there is agreement on a political or social/moral issue between them and someone else. Typically, statements were made regarding how they (as individuals or a community of faith) deal with others who have different views on a similar topic or how they (as individuals or a community of faith) are treated and dealt with by those with different viewpoints. Clearly, these participants believed that because of their faith, they were ridiculed and marginalized by those who disagree with them. An example of this sentiment was a comment made by a middle-aged man: "I believe a lot of times when there's [an] issue we feel is immoral and we'll speak up and say, God's word says this about that issue. But all of a sudden it's thrown in our face, 'you're intolerant, you're being intolerant, you're a hater.' I love the person I'm speaking to, but I love them as Christ does, but there's an area that you are in that God does not like and God loves you. But a lot of people turn that around and say that you are intolerant and they turn away and start bashing you."

This was one of several comments regarding what these participants believe was the unwillingness of others to accommodate their views and positions within the public square of ideas without "bashing" them for their faith-based positions. In fact, two participants related stories from their workplace. They detailed that because their political positions differed from the majority of those with whom they work, they felt pressured to keep quiet; otherwise, if they spoke up, they would suffer retribution. Therefore, these individuals clearly believed their rights to freedom of conscience were being stifled or outright denied. This type of circumstance was particularly evident in the example given by the man who was in the steel workers' union for 30 years. He stated that, "There were conflicts, moral conflicts with myself and some of the union leaders. I said, 'I really don't care for you to spend my money, my union dollars to support these certain candidates.' . . . They basically said 'we know what we are doing, so shut up. We'll do what we think is right with your money and you better vote for them if you want to work for a living'."

One very compelling argument was put forth by one of the participants. After hearing some of the troubles and feedback from others, he cast a positive light on these types of conflicts by stating, "That's why this country is great because you can have those conflicts." The point of his statement was that, regardless of the fact that everyone's situation may not be perfect as it relates to having their ideas respected or treated equitably, the fact that tension and conflict is allowed to take place in our society was viewed as a good thing. He went on, "You know that lady, that Chinese lady that yelled at the Chinese premier . . . you know the fortunate thing is that she has the freedom to say that [here in the United States]. . . those people who believe like she does in China . . . [would be] rounded up and shot and killed because they don't have that freedom."

Catholic

Another issue raised in this focus group, similar to the evangelical protestants, was that the Catholic participants had a very real sense that the Catholic Church and the Catholic faith tended to get attacked for positions on social and moral issues. Furthermore, the perception was that these attacks were very visible because of the size of the Church (e.g., because the Catholic Church is prominent worldwide, it can be easily targeted). However, when speaking about specific instances in which political tolerance might come into play, these participants spoke about not wanting to be in a position to judge others and not wanting to be judged by others. For example, one participant raised objections to the "targeting" of political candidates. She said, "They target candidates. When are they going to target us individually? [They tell candidates] you can't receive communion if you're pro-choice. And I think that's wrong." Another individual stated, "All of a sudden, some Cardinal didn't like John Kerry, because John Kerry's a Catholic. But the non-Catholic can take any stance they want, and there's no repercussion. But only the Catholic in elected office or campaigning for elected office is the target." An interesting aspect of this last comment is that the targeting of Catholics either in office or running for office, according to the example given, was done by others in an official church capacity, such as a cardinal refusing communion to John Kerry, and not by a non-Catholic.

Mainline Protestant

For these focus group participants, there were three themes discussed regarding political tolerance. The first was that Christians are at a disadvantage vis-à-vis others on the world stage. An example of this is exemplified by the following comment:

> Just being a Christian, and the concept of [that] kind of love and tolerance, puts us at a disadvantage when you're talking about international issues of combat. We can go home on our TV sets and have 100 depictions of things that we would find distasteful as Christians, with Jesus and representations of that. Yet there is one cartoon and all of a sudden the whole world is up in arms, and there are threats to people. We won't respond with concepts of terror, so therefore, we make an easy target; sometimes we are an easy target because of the fundamental values that we hold.

The second theme regarding political tolerance was that participants expressed a tangible sense of wrestling with how best to accommodate profound disagreements, particularly when those disagreements are rooted in religious worldviews. This is highlighted by one participant who discussed the need for "sensitivity to other faiths":

> Other faith is a part of what we're founded and based on. How do you do that [have sensitivity to other faiths]? How do you create Christian values and keep Christian values going when you have other denominations coming into the national mix? How do you keep from insulting that and continuing forward? At the same time, we want the original values that were thought of by our forefathers to be entrenched in our democracy.

Another individual stated, "I don't know if we'll ever have a total consensus on how to disagree and yet stand for what you believe firmly and yet disagree in love when there is room for disagreement."

The final theme discussed among this particular focus group was the belief that some of the most problematic attacks on Christianity come from within Christianity not from without. A very specific example was given as it related to this individual's specific denomination. He said:

> About twelve years ago, our youth pastor took a group of our youth to a Sunday worship [at a different congregation from within the same denomination], and the chaplain had a beard and long hair and that became the topic of the sermon that morning. How men should look like men. And God did not intend for men to be clean shaven. So the attacks come from within Christianity . . . the denomination.

Although both congregations were of the same denomination, one stressed the appropriateness of the outward appearance of men while the other did not. Therefore, the fact that this became an issue in the sermon was perceived as an attack on the visiting congregation that did not adhere to the same standards advocated in the sermon.

Church and State

In each focus group session, all participants were asked about the relationship between church and state, and much of the discussion and commentary made about it more accurately fits into a discussion of religion and politics. There were a few comments regarding "rendering to Caesar what is Caesar's and to God what is God's," but no explicit discussion occurred regarding institutional separation. In fact, I would argue that the institutional separation of church and state—no government control over religion; no institutional religious control over government—was assumed to exist. And not only was it assumed to exist, but it was implicitly assumed to be an accepted and preferred aspect of American democracy. The basis of the conversation was about the limits and boundaries between church and state and how that relationship plays out in individual lives and their communities. Thus, no focus group advocated or even expressed an implicit desire for institutional religious authority to be the sole basis of political authority. Rather, religious influence in America was to come about as individuals of faith participated in civic and political life, playing by the same rules as everyone else.

Black Protestant

These focus group participants, predominately, discussed the relationship between church and state as it related to political figures and election campaigns. That was not the only content of the discussion, but it certainly was the most extensively mentioned aspect of the relationship. Furthermore, many of the comments were not positive. There was a general discontent about the belief that politicians and candidates running for office used the church to get votes but ignored the electorate otherwise. One woman stated, "We have the politicians that want to come into the morning worship and greet or speak to the congregation. First of all, I think that is totally disrespectful. I haven't seen you in twelve months. . . . You haven't done anything for the city; you haven't done anything in this position. Now you show up on Sunday morning, begging for me to vote for you."

Although no one disagreed with the notion of a separation of church and state, it was clear that quite a few participants did not believe that there is, can be, or ever will be total separation. In fact, one participant explicitly stated, "In my mind, that was never the intent of the founding fathers [to have absolute separation]. . . . Everything . . . from the beginning was built on those two being together." Thus, there is a sentiment toward a natural, even necessary and valued, relationship between church and state; but no one expressed any sentiment that could be interpreted as advocating greater church control over civil society. In contrast, the expressions were of the need for righteous men and women to occupy positions of authority within the civil government. This sentiment was stated as, "I think they should be separate because, I think, when righteous men and women govern, then [it] will work." In essence, "the righteous and just people will do what's for the good of the country." So we do not need to have church and state intertwined, what we need, as a country, is for righteous people to hold positions in government.

Evangelical Protestant

These focus group participants, in comparison to the others, expressed the greatest range of ideas concerning the relationship between church and state. There was a general consensus around one central theme, but there were two ideas—from two different individuals—that fell at opposite ends of the spectrum regarding this topic. Regarding the ideas that were, in essence, polar opposites, the first was from a young woman of college age who said, "I agree with the separation of state and church probably, I am encouraged by it, like it seems like a lot of people my age, if you are really strong in your faith, you can find ways to share your faith. . . . It makes me work harder because if it wasn't hard then what would I really do? If you really want something that bad, it will happen." Thus, we have a young woman indicating that guidelines governing the appropriate relationship between church and state actually make her work harder to share her faith with others. That challenge is a source of motivation that is not only accepted but preferred. On the opposite end of the spectrum, was an individual who did not believe that a strict separation of church and state was beneficial. He stated:

> If we were just free as we were at the beginning for religion to be debated on the state level and maybe say the government schools, public schools, if those things were free to be debated, presented, used in those schools, I have no doubt that Christianity would, if you want to call it, win out. Christianity and Judaism, these are altruistic religions, these are things that are based on serving your fellow man and those organizations would flourish. . . . But the state limits those freedoms, freedom of speech, freedom of religion, in what we call the government zone, they are not allowed to flourish so they have to go to a secular view. So they are creating a problem, they are creating so many more problems by restricting people's freedom.

To add to the diversity of thought on this topic, yet another man, in thinking about the relationship between church and state as separate, he said, "Well, that's sort of healthy, because if I was a minority, if Christianity was a minority in this country and it was some other religious group that was total opposite of me, I probably wouldn't want them to have all access to government and me not."

Yet, it was clear that quite a few participants in this focus group had a real sense of combat in the workplace; that is, they believed that they had to hide their beliefs and their faith to comply with a strict separation of church and state. One woman, who worked as a counselor for the local government said, "For me, the separation of church and state is coming into an everyday battle every time I go to work. One of the things they say [is] if a client brings it up, then you're free to respond but don't you speak first." Another young woman, a teacher in the public school, made the point "I work in one of the public schools. One of the artists did very little else than Christian or religious art. I was warned that I better be careful how I presented the artwork; I couldn't speak of the faith of the man, nothing about that, but I can talk about Edgar Allen Poe's suicide." Finally, one of the participants who worked at the church complained:

> They will leave her [the government counselor] and then go to a church because the local township that they went to, to get help from, has a list of churches, and they say, "now you go to the church to get help from the church." And so [they are] basically referred by the government to the church and the church helps them out with their food and their rent and their [utility] bills, all those type of things. But when we turn around and we try to be involved in a more fervent level, we have someone standing there saying you are not welcome in the door because you are a religious organization. That's the tension that the church has to deal with.

Catholic

For these focus group participants, the perception exists that the separation of church and state concept has been and is being used against the Catholic Church and that media and certain commentators in the media have been attacking the Catholic Church. In particular, one participant said, "If you paid much attention to Lou Dobbs . . . over the last month or two. He is mercilessly attacking the Catholic faith and their federal tax exempt status." The sense was that the Church, in general, has a role to play in contributing to public debate and dialogue in this country, yet, when it does so, it is attacked. The same individual said, for the church to speak up means "we're just going to get walked over politically every which way." Putting this problem into historical perspective, as well as adding another dimension to why the Catholic church is a target of attack, another participant talked about how, when John F. Kennedy was running for president in 1960, "the rumor [was] the United States is going to be ruled from Rome. . . . That was the perception because we are a powerful body, we have financial means, and so we may be perceived . . . as a greater threat." Furthermore, there was a real concern that our country had, sadly, drifted away from its original underpinning in which faith was considered a valued part of democracy, a valued part of the establishment of this country. One statement to this regard was "they got divided in the verbiage . . . but it was founded on faith." Finally, for one individual, the role of the Church was of extreme importance. He said, "The state is a mess. Who's going pull it together if it isn't faith and God?"

Mainline Protestant

The overwhelming sentiment from this session was that although there is, in the United States, a type of separation of church and state, the separation is not concrete and the line between the two is often invisible. There was a general concern that, in contemporary times, the quest for an absolute separation of church and state has eroded—or downplayed—the role of faith and values as central elements in the founding of our country and central to the motivations of many of our country's forefathers. In fact, the former Soviet Union was used as an example of what happens (in the negative sense) when faith and religion are excluded from a society. One participant indicated that he keeps "crisscrossing" the line between church and state "as an individual who has faith." He went on to argue:

> There are two definitions within me as a person to differentiate, how do Americans look at that? There is the intellectual part of Americans, what they are taught and what they learn in civic classes, in U.S. history classes, that teaches the actual separation of church and state . . . . Going from the intellectual to the practical, we knew full and well, all of us, that the president going to church on Sunday morning is sending a message. Congress starting with a prayer is sending a message, having a Memorial Day worship service has a message, having chaplains in the military, in the police and sheriff departments, these are all messages that are the practical part of society of the American life that is being sent out.

No one suggested that they did not want institutional separation of church and state. In fact, one individual even talked about how "most of the world, they don't separate the two [church and state]." And this individual related that comment in relationship to our current involvement in the Middle East stating that there is a perception by those within the Middle East that "it's these Christians . . . [not] those are the policies of the United States."

There were two church and state problems explicitly mentioned. In an interesting statement, one problem mentioned had to do with Congress. An individual complained that many members of Congress try to look pious and they go along with starting congressional sessions with a prayer, but then "when they get into their business . . . they're only out for themselves." In the second instance, the problem was one of too much involvement by a church when such involvement is "right in the church center itself." This particular participant went on to say, "Give people the conscience and the faith and the values to make their own choices."

Summary

This chapter related how the use of focus groups in Lake County, Indiana, provided an examination of four central themes: faith and citizenship, faith-based issues, political tolerance, and the relationship between church and state. This summary on the theme of liberal democracy will include an explicit discussion of political tolerance. To begin, none of the focus groups discussed political tolerance as it is defined by academicians in political science. This remained true even after political tolerance was defined for each group. Political tolerance is important to liberal democracy. If we want to take advantage of the benefits of focus group research—a technique that allows for participants to express their views and beliefs in an unstructured format—and add subjective context to the empirical, objective data, then a better means of structuring the conversation must take place. In this instance, casting a broad net and having the moderator employ a less-structured format did not enable me to concretely bring data to bear on thoughts, beliefs, attitudes, and perceptions as they related to political tolerance, at least in a direct, empirical sense. In the empirical data examined in chapter 2, there were specific political tolerance questions that asked respondents about their willingness to let someone from their most-disliked group run for public office, teach in public schools, make a public speech, and hold public rallies. By not specifically engaging those types of questions as they relate to political tolerance, I am not able to speak specifically to those precise political tolerance questions.

Nevertheless, there is important information that can be gleaned from the conversation that did take place. For example, the explicit feedback elicited from the black protestant participants in the discussion of political tolerance was dominated by a strict political focus regarding Republicans and Democrats. This suggests an implicit recognition that political tolerance does indeed involve groups and individuals with competing perspectives with which one does not agree. There was also a very apparent recognition that a diverse society with diverse perspectives must find a way to accommodate views different from an individual's own without shutting those views out of the public square. The mainline protestant focus group grappled with finding a means of balancing profound disagreements within a pluralist society. Speaking to the issue of political tolerance, this group maintained an implicit recognition that disagreements, sometimes very difficult and contentious disagreements, do exist and that some means of handling these disagreements must be maintained. For the evangelical protestant, this implicit recognition was also very apparent, although it was presented in a different context. When their responses to political tolerance are reviewed, this group clearly indicated a sense that they felt pressured to keep their views to themselves, and they clearly did not think that such pressure was appropriate. Thus, there is a recognition that putting a group or individual into a position where their basic freedom to present their views is negated is a problem. Although I cannot specifically relate this to the objective political tolerance items in terms of these participants' willingness to extend civil liberties to those with whom they disagree, it is clear that they have a sense that those who disagree with them are engaging in behavior that is counter to political tolerance.

Because these focus groups cast a broad net in terms of content, I am able to use them as a means of addressing the argument of Kraynak (2001), who argued that Christians in the contemporary United States do not just prefer liberal democracy to other systems of governance, but they actually perceive liberal democracy as a God-ordained system. Furthermore, they welcome "modern liberal democracy as a friend and an ally, even though they may criticize some of its features as misguided or downright immoral" (2001, 167).

I believe that an objective assessment of these focus groups demonstrates a commitment to liberal democratic politics across all four sets of participants. As mentioned previously, the discussion related to the relationship between church and state did not produce any feedback from any of the four sets of participants that indicated a preference for formal religious authority over the current American secular government. This is important because it suggests that the members of these four different congregations have all been socialized into an acceptance of and preference for a liberal democratic form of government; which is to say, a government not controlled by a particular religious authority—just what Kraynak (2001) argues.

In addition, it is clear in all four focus group sessions that the participants viewed their participation in civic society as consistent with their faith and that the dominant means by which faith influences civic society was for individuals to take their faith and values into the political marketplace. An important aspect of this reality to be stressed is that these individuals view themselves as legitimate participants in the process of liberal democratic decision-making. They consider their behavior as a normal and natural part of the liberal democratic system. For them, there is no disconnect between liberal democracy and positions and views informed by one's faith. This is the difference between religion and politics and church and state. No focus group participant explicitly distinguished, conceptually, between religion and politics versus church and state, but it is clear that the manner in which the relationship between church and state was discussed was, at the individual behavioral level, indicative of religion and politics versus the institutional (and structural) relationship between church and state.

What these focus groups demonstrate—consistent with the arguments not only of Kraynak (2001, 167) but also of Wolfe (2002, 255)—is that "[r]eligious believers blend into the modern American landscape." The religious individuals among us are, in the aggregate, not against liberal democracy. Rather, they grapple with issues of political tolerance, and far from expressing a desire to eliminate other views from the marketplace of ideas, they focus instead on participating in a civil society in which they can represent their views vis-à-vis others that they fully expect and accept will be in that marketplace with them. And, all four focus group participants showed Christian adherents to be willing to be self-reflective both individually and as a community of faith—evidenced by the candor with which they willingly criticized failings within their own particular faith group.

Consistent with the results from chapter 2, the results of these focus groups indicate that a reassessment is in order regarding the *a priori* assumption of an inherent conflict between religion and liberal democracy, in general, as well as religion and political tolerance, in particular. In fact, the research of Bolce and De Maio (1999a, 1999b) that was referenced at the beginning of this chapter certainly suggests that concerns regarding political tolerance are applicable to those outside the realm that has, typically, been of the most concern (e.g., the religiously committed, or the religious believer). Such a realization by itself does not negate any concern that may arise regarding the relationship between individuals of faith, liberal democracy, and political tolerance, but it does indicate concretely that one of the virtues of liberal democratic politics and political tolerance (or lack thereof) does not revolve uniquely around religion to the exclusion of the nonreligious (secular) or even the very educated.

Chapter 4

Issue Attitudes, Religion, and Political Tolerance

Private opinion creates public opinion. Public opinion overflows eventually into national behavior and national behavior, as things are arranged at present, can make or mar the world. That is why private opinion, and private behavior, and private conversation are so terrifyingly important.

—Jan Struther (Joyce Anstruther) in "The Weather of the World," from A Pocketful of Peebles, *1946, p. 341*

In the two previous chapters, I have attempted to draw a picture of the relationship between religion and political tolerance that is less toxic than has been depicted in academic and popular circles in regard to assessing the relationship between religion and political tolerance in the United States, in particular, and faith and democracy, in general. For example, the empirical data from chapter 2 and the qualitative data from chapter 3 support the contention that if one is concerned about political intolerance, religious commitment and religion generally are not the dominant arenas requiring reform. The empirical results in chapter 2 show that the strongest predictors of political tolerance are threat perception and support for the norms of democracy. Likewise, the qualitative results from chapter 3 indicate that liberal democracy is a valued and preferred system of governance by the religiously committed in the United States.

In this fourth chapter, I address the potential linkages between issue-attitude positions and political tolerance with a focus exclusively on three of the social and moral issues that are current hot-button topics in America—abortion, stem-cell research, and homosexual marriage. Because of the intense debate over these and other social and moral issues, a chapter addressing that debate is essential, if for no other reason, than that popular opinion, particularly as it relates to what can colloquially be called "conservative Christian right" attitudes toward abortion, stem-cell research, and homosexual marriage are often considered proof positive of political intolerance. Given the importance in our current political environment between hot-button political issue attitudes and perceptions of tolerance versus intolerance, empirical research examining the potential linkage between these attitudes and political tolerance is a necessary and important area of scholarship. I want to be clear that this chapter is merely an introductory look at the trisection of religion, public opinion, and political tolerance and is exploratory in nature. It is by no means a comprehensive consideration of the data.

To assess the relationship between issue-attitude positions (public opinion), religion, and political tolerance, this chapter uses a survey-based experimental design in which the "opinion assessment technique is systematically manipulated" (Kinder & Palfrey 1993, 13). Specifically, I use surveys in which I manipulate the question wording as it relates to abortion, stem-cell research, and homosexual marriage; questions on these three particular topics are asked in three different types of contexts: social, neutral, and moral (all other questions in the surveys are identical). By manipulating the context in which questions on these three issues are asked, I can asses whether or not moral opposition to abortion, stem-cell research, or homosexual marriage results in less political tolerance (the expected result based on previous research) than those asked about these same issues in a neutral or social context. Differences can also be assessed regarding political tolerance between the social, neutral, and moral contexts by religious tradition and religious commitment.

Religion and Political Behavior

There is a general scholarly consensus that the 1976 presidential candidacy of Jimmy Carter, a born-again Southern Baptist Christian, marked the modern ascent of what we now term the Religious Right or Christian Right movement. Carter's candidacy is said to have signaled to the Christian community the acceptability of mixing religion with politics (Wilcox, 2000). In the aftermath of this, the Moral Majority was founded in 1979 with Jerry Falwell, and Pat Robertson came into prominence in the following decade. Thus, it was during the late 1970s that scholarly interest started to turn toward the impact of religion in politics. Since then, the literature in this arena has grown rapidly. Regardless of the reasons for the increase of research in the area of religion and politics, it has long been recognized that when studying mass political attitudes that "religious differentiation intrudes on partisan political alignments in [an] unexpectedly powerful degree wherever it conceivably can" (Converse 1974, 734). Considering that religion is a dominant and enduring aspect of the American landscape, its tradition, and its people; and with the conclusions drawn from the empirical and qualitative data from the previous chapters, I begin this chapter with a brief overview of how religion in America impacts issue attitudes.

There is a sprawling array of literature on the relationship between religion and political behavior (e.g., presidential vote choice, levels of participation, partisanship, and social and moral issue attitudes), but for the purposes here, the literature most relevant is the literature within religion and public opinion. Many of the most contentious issues of our time involve social and moral attitude positions, such as prayer in school, abortion, education, gender roles, and homosexual rights.[1] Likewise, most of the public opinion literature has focused on the "most contentious issues" such as abortion and homosexual rights; much of this literature has focused on religious individuals, mainly evangelical protestants, Catholics, and mainline protestants (Olson & Jelen 1998).

In the bevy of studies that has analyzed attitudinal differences on social/moral issues among the various religious traditions (e.g., the belonging dimension of religion), there is a consensus of results. Identification with a religious tradition (e.g., denominational affiliation) is more likely to lead to increased social/moral conservatism than no identification with a religious tradition or a secular identification. Furthermore, members of some traditions, typically evangelical protestants, are more conservative than others such as Jewish or mainline protestant groups (Wald 2003, chap, 6). Conservatism on social/moral issues is also related to various indicators of religious commitment (e.g., the behavior dimension of religion) whether level of church attendance, level of devotionalism, other indicators of church involvement, and measures of religious salience.

In all instances, increased religious activity or commitment resulted in increased conservatism on many issues covering a broad range, including:

1. The Equal Rights Amendment, or ERA (Wilcox 1987; Layman 1997)
2. Abortion (Wilcox 1987; Jelen 1991, chap. 3; Guth, Smidt, Kellstedt & Green 1993; Leege et al. 1993; and Wald, Kellstedt & Leege 1993; Layman 1997; Layman & Green 1998, 14)
3. Discrimination against women in society (Wilcox 1987; Layman 1997)
4. Attitudes toward school prayer (Leege et al. 1993; Layman 1997; Layman & Green 1998, 14)
5. Gender roles (Wilcox 1987; Jelen 1991)

Thus, there is more than merely a general perception that increased religiosity (whether behavior or belonging) leads to more conservative social and moral issue attitudes. It is an empirical reality. This reality, however, does not reveal anything about how issue attitudes by themselves or in conjunction with religion relate to political tolerance. More often than not, the propensity for increased religiosity to lead to increased social/moral conservatism—particularly as it relates to the evangelical protestant tradition—is portrayed as having a detrimental if not fatal influence on political tolerance in particular and liberal democracy in general. All too often, religious individuals with very conservative social and moral issue-attitude positions have been purported to represent a threat to many individuals' notions of rights and liberties.

Nevertheless, it is quickly forgotten that political tolerance explicitly is not about acceptance of certain issue attitudes. Political tolerance is about the willingness to extend specific civil liberties (speech, petition, and assembly) to those with whom one disagrees.[2] And though it certainly is of interest and great import to study and assess the issue-attitude positions of religious adherents of all stripes, the aforementioned studies do not test for nor conclude that these conservative issue-attitude positions are in any way a threat to political tolerance. Yet, the perception that conservative issue-attitude positions represent a detrimental or fatal influence as they relate to our most basic rights and liberties is the mainstream conclusion when presented with such information. The point here is that a generally accepted perception holds that those who have conservative social/moral issue-attitude positions (regarding homosexual marriage and abortion, for example) have less political tolerance than those whose views are more liberal.

Religion, Issue Attitudes, and Political Tolerance: A Survey-Based Experiment

This chapter addresses several questions. The first is: How is opposition to abortion, stem-cell research, and/or homosexual marriage influenced by context (e.g., social, neutral, or moral)? It is important to distinguish between a moral and a social context regarding these issue-attitude positions. As can be seen from the qualitative focus group results in chapter 3, some Christian adherents—particularly those from the evangelical protestant tradition—routinely make distinctions between opposition to issues (such as abortion and homosexual marriage) based on moral considerations (such as behavior that is considered contrary to godliness or that is against the moral strictures ordained by God), while simultaneously arguing that their opposition regards the behavior and not the individual per se. One's opposition to abortion and homosexual marriage is opposition to the immoral behavior, not to the person committing the behavior. Fulton, Gorsuch, and Maynard (1999) conducted a study in which they differentiated between attitudes toward homosexuals that were moral (e.g., the behavior of homosexuality is perverted) and nonmoral (e.g., support for discrimination against homosexuals in housing or employment).[3] Drawing on this line of distinction, I constructed questions regarding opposition to abortion, stem-cell research, and homosexual marriage that differentiated between opposition to these issues based on moral grounds, in contrast to a general opposition (e.g., a neutral context) or a social opposition. Given the previous literature regarding the relationship between increased religiosity and conservative issue attitudes, greater moral opposition to these issues is anticipated.

The second question addressed in this chapter is: Does the interaction of context and religion influence issues attitude (e.g., level of opposition or lack thereof) toward abortion, stem-cell research, and/or homosexual marriage? Given the previous literature, I anticipate that religious commitment will influence issue-attitude position; in addition, I anticipate that greater influence will be attached to those associated with the evangelical protestant tradition. The final question addressed in this chapter is: Does the interaction of context and issue attitude (e.g., level of opposition) influence political tolerance? Because of the prominence of social/moral issues in the political arena, this is an important aspect and distinction to assess. If popular perception regarding conservative issue-attitude positions and political tolerance is believed, then those with high levels of moral opposition to the issue attitudes under investigation here will result in lower levels of political tolerance.

Data and Methods

To assess the three questions in this chapter, I conducted a survey-based experiment on political attitudes, with a particular focus on abortion, stem-cell research, and homosexual marriage. In the survey, I manipulated the context by presenting questions regarding "level of opposition" to abortion, stem-cell research, and homosexual marriage in three different contexts: social, neutral, and moral. During Fall 2005, 220 subjects (which were college students, hereafter referred to as "students") were selected from several 100-level introductory social science courses (American government, sociology, and psychology) at a regional campus of a large state-funded university. Each student was randomly assigned to one of three context groups (social, neutral, and moral) and given a questionnaire for completion. The questionnaires, given to all 220 students, were identical except for the questions regarding abortion, stem-cell research and homosexual marriage.[4]

In one version of the survey, the questions about these three issues were presented without either a social or a moral context. That is, opposition to abortion, stem-cell research, and homosexual marriage was presented in a "neutral" context (e.g., no connotations of moral or social ramifications). In the second version of the survey, the three questions on opposition to abortion, stem-cell research and homosexual marriage were asked in a societal context (e.g., opposition to these issues was asked with specific negative societal ramifications). Finally, in the third version of the survey, the three questions were asked in a moral context (e.g., opposition to these issues was asked with specific negative moral ramifications). Of the 220 students, 76 received the survey asking about issue attitudes in a social context, 72 received the survey asking about issue attitudes in a neutral context, and 72 were administered the survey that asked the issue-attitude questions in a moral context. All questions were a 5-point Likert scale ranging from 1 (strongly agree) to 5 (strongly disagree). A low score indicates opposition to abortion, stem-cell research and homosexual marriage, and a high score indicates no or low levels of opposition to these three topics. For example, if someone strongly agrees with a question in a moral context, such as "Homosexual marriage should not be allowed because it goes against God," then their opposition to homosexual marriage is considered a moral opposition.

Table 4.1

ISSUE ATTITUDE QUESTION WORDING

Social Context (n = 76)	1. Homosexual marriage should not be allowed because it disrupts society. 2. Stem-cell research should not be allowed because it is dangerous to society. 3. Abortion should not be allowed because it is damaging to society.
Neutral Context (n = 72)	1. Homosexual marriage should not be allowed. 2. Stem-cell research should not be allowed. 3. Abortion should not be allowed.
Moral Context (n = 72)	1. Homosexual marriage should not be allowed because it goes against God. 2. Stem-cell research should not be allowed because it is morally wrong. 3. Abortion should not be allowed because it destroys life.

Of course, the use of college students as subjects in a survey-based experiment creates potential problems for generalizing results. It is recognized that the subject pool is not perfectly representative of the American public at large. Therefore, my results must be taken with the knowledge that the subjects are not an accurate reflection of the mass public. However, the demographics of the sample were generally similar to those of the population in Lake County, Indiana regarding racial makeup and reported family income.[5] Thus, my results should not be dismissed simply on the basis of the "college sophomore" argument and can still be used to understand the relationship between some of the most hotly contested social/moral issue attitudes and political tolerance.

Results—Does Context Matter?

The first question, stated previously, is whether opposition to abortion, stem-cell research, and homosexual marriage is influenced by context (social, neutral, and/or moral). I expected to find that respondents would register greater opposition to these issues when asked about them in a moral context versus a neutral or social context. To determine whether opposition to these issue attitudes is influenced by context, I used a one-way analysis of variance.[6] My stated expectations were met only for the issue of abortion. There was greater opposition to abortion when presented in a moral context than when presented in a social or a neutral context (remember, the lower the score, the greater the opposition).

As can be seen from the mean scores across the three different context groups in figure 4.1 (3.72 social context; 3.47 neutral context; 3.14 moral context), the mean scores for the social and neutral contexts reflected less opposition to abortion than the mean score attributed to the moral context. Furthermore, the difference between the means for attitudes toward abortion when presented in a moral versus a social or neutral context is statistically significant. The F statistic for this analysis is 2.996 (p. = .052). Specifically, the statistically significant difference is between the context groups that answered issue attitudes presented in a social context versus those who answered the issue-attitude questions in a moral context. However, the eta-squared for the ability of context to explain attitudes toward abortion is a weak 2.6 percent (.026 calculated by subtracting the residual sum of squares from the total sum of squares and dividing by the total sum of squares: 472.450–459.753/472.450 = .026).[7]

Figure 4.1
Mean Abortion Score by Context*

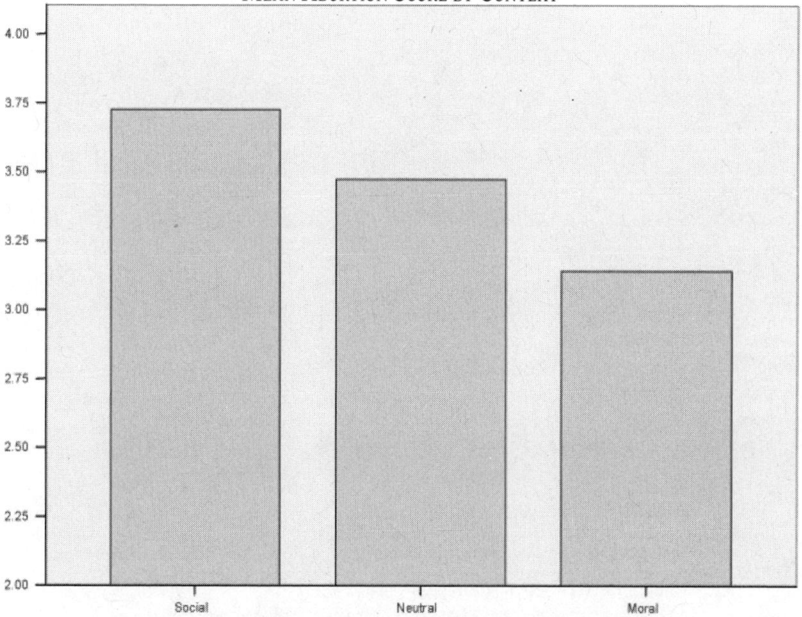

*Responses were coded 1 = Strongly agree; 2 = Agree; 3 = Neither agree or disagree; 4 = Disagree; 5 = Strongly disagree

In contrast to the abortion issue attitude, context did not matter for stem-cell research and homosexual marriage. For the issue attitude concerning stem-cell research, there is no substantive or statistical difference between the social, neutral, and moral contexts. The mean score for the social context group was 3.53; for the neutral context group, it was 3.50; and for the moral context group, it was 3.62. Furthermore, the F statistic for the analysis of variance pertaining to stem-cell research is extremely low at .182 ($p = .834$). The results for the homosexual marriage issue attitude are similar. As can be seen from the mean scores across the three different context groups (3.36 social context; 3.32 neutral context; 3.35 moral context), subjects' scores reflected no substantive differences. Similarly, there was also no statistically significant results to report; the F statistic for the analysis of variance for the homosexual marriage issue attitude is, for all practical purposes, nonexistent at .011 ($p = .989$).

Figure 4.2

Mean Stem Cell Research by Context*

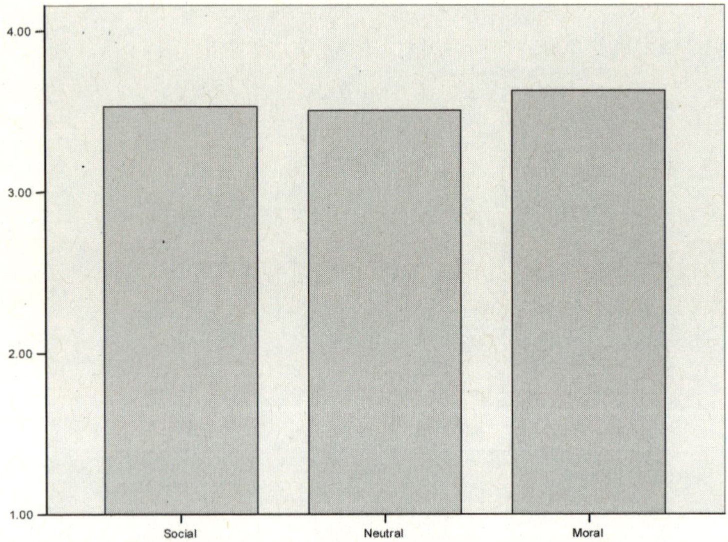

*Responses were coded 1 = Strongly agree; 2 = Agree; 3 = Neither agree or disagree; 4 = Disagree; 5 = Strongly disagree

Figure 4.3

Mean Homosexual Marriage Score by Context*

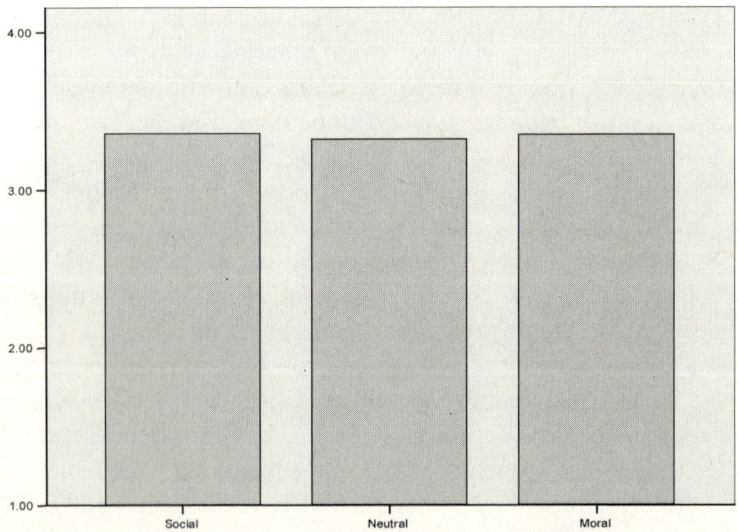

*Responses were coded 1 = Strongly agree; 2 = Agree; 3 = Neither agree or disagree; 4 = Disagree; 5 = Strongly disagree

In the aggregate, these findings demonstrate little to no support for the role of a social, neutral, or moral context to influence issue-attitude positions on these three hot-button issues in the contemporary United States. Nevertheless, given the importance of religion in this debate and the centrality of religion to the topic of this book, the next analysis undertaken specifically incorporates religion.

Does Context by Religion Matter? Testing for an Interaction Effect

The second question of the chapter involves the interaction of context and religion and how this might influence issue attitudes (e.g., level of opposition or lack thereof) toward abortion, stem-cell research, and/or homosexual marriage. To address this question, I used a factorial Analysis of Variance (or ANOVA) design to enable the use of multiple predictor/factor variables. In this instance, those multiple predictor variables are context (social, neutral, moral) and religious tradition (evangelical protestant, mainline protestant, black protestant, and Catholic).[8] Essentially, I test for the interaction effect of context and religious tradition (e.g., cross-tabulating predictor categories) on issue attitude (e.g., level of opposition or lack thereof) toward abortion, stem-cell research, and homosexual marriage. I also incorporate as a covariate the interval-level religious commitment variable (refer to question 5 in section B of Appendix F: Political Attitudes Questionnaire for the specific question wording and measurement of religious commitment), which means that I am testing for the influence of context and religious tradition on issue attitude, taking into account the level of religious commitment.[9] One important point is that the factorial ANOVA does not provide information regarding whether specific means are significantly different from one another; it simply indicates whether or not a significant interaction between the two predictor variables (context and religious tradition) exist and whether or not the covariate—religious commitment—explains any of the variance in issue attitude.[10]

As a review of table 4.2 shows, the factorial ANOVA for the abortion, stem-cell research, and homosexual marriage issue attitudes demonstrated weak to very weak overall results. The model with the best overall explanatory power, the issue attitude of abortion, resulted in the two predictor variables and the interval-level covariate explaining 20.2 percent of the variance for the model as a whole (.202 is the value of the eta squared for the model as a whole).

Table 4.2
FACTORIAL ANOVA DESIGN
(CONTEXT BY RELIGIOUS TRADITION WITH RELIGIOUS COMMITMENT)

Issue Attitude	*Predictor Variables*	*Sum of Squares*	*F*	*Significance*	*Eta-Squared*
Abortion	Context	13.989	3.973	.021	.040
	Tradition	8.047	1.524	.211	.023
	Religious Commitment	40.686	23.109	.000	.117
	Tradition-by-Context	7.441	.704	.647	.021
Total Sum of Squares = 347.425; F = 3.611; Significance = .000; Eta-Squared = .202					
Stem-Cell Research	Context	2.760	.825	.440	.009
	Tradition	2.733	.545	.652	.009
	Religious Commitment	9.103	5.446	.021	.032
	Tradition-by-Context	8.844	.882	.510	.031
Total Sum of Squares = 283.497; F = 1.300; Significance = .224; Eta-Squared = .083					
Homosexual Marriage	Context	.456	.108	.898	.001
	Tradition	15.633	2.467	.064	.040
	Religious Commitment	8.252	3.906	.050	.021
	Tradition-by-Context	26.838	2.118	.054	.069
Total Sum of Squares = 386.874; F = 2.429; Significance = .006; Eta-Squared = .132					

Explained variance under 25 percent is considered a weak result. The eta-squared for stem-cell research and homosexual marriage (for the model as a whole) was even lower with 8.3 percent of the variance explained and 13.2 percent of the variance explained by the predicator variables and covariate (religious commitment), respectively. For the abortion and homosexual marriage issue attitudes, the models overall were statistically significant, but the overall model for stem-cell research was not statistically significant. However, religious commitment (the covariate in all three models) did have statistically significant contributions to the explained variance of each respective issue attitude. In similar fashion to the explained variance for the overall model, the explained variance attributable to religious commitment is very weak for stem-cell research and homosexual marriage (3.2 percent and 2.1 percent, respectively), and a weak 11.7 percent for the abortion issue attitude.

Because the factorial ANOVA enables us to determine whether or not there is a significant interaction between the two predictor variables of context and religious tradition, it is important to examine the results of that specific interaction. The only model in which this interaction had any influence was for the homosexual marriage issue attitude, being the only model in which that specific interaction was statistically significant. The interaction variable of context by religious tradition explained 6.9 percent of the variance in that model. In the analyses of abortion and stem-cell research, the interaction variable was not statistically significant (and the explanatory power of the interaction variable for both the analysis of abortion and stem-cell research was extremely weak).

Remember, the factorial ANOVA allows us to determine whether an interaction exists, but it does not tell us between what groups it exists, which means that it does not tell us what specific means differ from one another. To address which specific means are significantly different from one another, I computed a one-way ANOVA, which required creating a single predictor variable from context and religious tradition. The new variable had twelve levels, each of which consisted of a unique combination of context (social, neutral, and moral) by religious tradition (Catholic, black protestant, mainline protestant, and evangelical protestant).[11] Because the homosexual marriage issue attitude was the only analysis that resulted in statistically significant results for the interaction variable, I only report the results of the one-way ANOVA for that particular issue attitude.[12]

Table 4.3
Context by Religious Tradition (As a Single Predictor Varible)

Context	*Religious Tradition*	*Mean: Homosexual Marriage*	*Statistically Significant Difference of Means (.05)*
Social	Catholic	3.42	
	Black Protestant	2.90	
	Mainline Protestant	3.40	
	Evangelical Protestant	3.08	
Neutral	Catholic	3.96	Mainline Protestant/ Catholic
	Black Protestant	2.87	Black Protestant/ Catholic
	Mainline Protestant	2.13	Mainline Protestant/ Evangelical
	Evangelical Protestant	3.64	
Moral	Catholic	3.67	Catholic/ Evangelical
	Black Protestant	2.85	
	Mainline Protestant	3.78	Mainline Protestant/ Evangelical
	Evangelical Protestant	2.00	

Within the neutral context (e.g., those who were administered the questions on homosexual marriage presented in a neutral fashion), table 4.3 shows a statistically significant difference between the mean issue-attitude scores of Catholics and mainline protestants, black protestants and Catholics, and between mainline protestants and evangelical protestants. For the results within the moral context, the mean issue-attitude scores had a statistically significant difference between Catholics and evangelical protestants as well as between mainline protestants and evangelical protestants. In table 4.4, I provide all the mean scores for each religious tradition, by context, for the three issue attitudes. Using a one-way ANOVA, similar to the one conducted for the information provided in table 4.3, I was able to learn whether or not specific means across the three contexts (social, neutral, and moral) were significantly different from one another regarding each religious tradition separately and individually; that is, does the mean issue-attitude score for Catholics, mainliners, and evangelicals differ depending on the social, neutral, or moral context?

Table 4.4
MEAN ISSUE ATTITUDE SCORES (TRADITION BY CONTEXT)

Religious Tradition	*Context*	*Mean: Abortion*	*Mean: Stem-Cell Research*	*Mean: Homosexual Marriage*	*N*
Catholic	Social	3.67	3.71	3.42	24
	Neutral	3.80	3.60	3.96	25
	Moral	3.33	3.92	3.67	24
Black Protestant	Social	3.60	3.30	2.90	10
	Neutral	2.73	3.13	2.87	15
	Moral	2.77	3.15	2.85	13
Mainline Protestant	Social	3.80	3.20	3.40	5
	Neutral	3.75	4.37	2.12	8
	Moral	3.11	3.33	3.78	9
Evangelical Protestant	Social	3.00	3.23	3.08	13
	Neutral	3.45	3.54	3.63	11
	Moral	3.20	3.50	2.00	10

For the Catholic and black protestant traditions regarding abortion, stem-cell research, and homosexual marriage, the mean scores did not have statistically significant differences of means across the three contexts. For the mainline protestants, there was a statistically significant difference of means for the mean scores regarding homosexual marriage, and the statistically significant difference was between those mainline protestants in the neutral group and the mainline protestants in the moral group. Similarly for the evangelical protestants, there was a statistically significant difference of means for the mean score as it relates to homosexual marriage; again, the statistically significant difference was between those evangelical protestants in the neutral group and the evangelical protestants in the moral group. There were no other statistically significant differences of means found for the mainline protestants or evangelical protestants.

As indicated previously in this chapter, there is a relationship between religious belonging (e.g., religious tradition) and religious behavior (e.g., religious commitment) that is an empirical reality, as the results presented earlier further reaffirm and support. However, also stated previously in this chapter was the empirical reality of the relationship between religion (belonging and behavior) and issue attitudes that do not tell us anything about how these issue-attitude positions (by themselves or in conjunction with religion) relate to political tolerance. That specific linkage is addressed in the following section.

Issue Attitude and Political Tolerance: Is There a Link?

In this final analysis, I want to begin an examination of the potential connection between issue-attitude positions and political tolerance. Therefore, I am attempting to assess whether or not the social, neutral, or moral context of abortion, stem-cell research, and homosexual marriage has any influence on political tolerance. My first order of business is to discuss my political tolerance variable. My definition and conceptualization of political tolerance for this analysis is the same as I articulated in chapter 1. Likewise, my measurement of political tolerance is based on the least-liked content-controlled measurement design developed by Sullivan, Piereson, and Marcus (1982), which was also discussed in chapter 1 (and its measurement discussed explicitly in chap. 2). Therefore, I will not review the least-liked content-controlled approach to measuring political tolerance.[13] In this chapter, political tolerance is measured by four Likert scale questions.[14] Each of the four statements has a five-point scale ranging from 1 (strongly agree) to 5 (strongly disagree). I then construct a cumulative scale from the four political tolerance questions shown in table 4.5. Please see Appendix F for a copy of the survey used for this chapter's analyses, which includes the measurement of political tolerance.

Table 4.5
POLITICAL TOLERANCE

1. [Least-Liked Group] should be banned from running for public office in the United States.
2. [Least-Liked Group] should be allowed to teach in public schools.
3. [Least-Liked Group] should be outlawed.
4. [Least-Liked Group] should be allowed to hold public rallies.

At the beginning of this chapter, I explicitly stated that my intent was to examine whether any linkage exists between issue-attitude positions and political tolerance. To begin to understand this potential linkage, I have used the current hot-button topics of abortion, stem-cell research, and homosexual marriage. Furthermore, I have thus far assessed whether or not the context in which these issues are discussed matters by asking about them in a social, neutral, and moral context. I must now bring political tolerance into the analysis. Substantively, this means that issue-attitude score is no longer my dependent variable, as it had been in the previous analyses in this chapter. Political tolerance is now the dependent variable and issue attitude now becomes a predictor variable. Because of the perception (at least in American popular culture) that the issue attitudes of conservative Christians tend them toward intolerance, one might, therefore, expect that the evangelical Christians who agree with the questions regarding abortion, stem-cell research, and homosexual marriage (see table 4.1), particularly when asked in a moral context versus a social or neutral context, will have less political tolerance than others. Such considerations are exactly what I attempt to get at in this section.

To conduct this analysis, I used a factorial ANOVA in which I cross-tabulate the two predictor variables (or factors) of context (social, neutral, moral) by issue attitude on political tolerance. Because religious tradition provided so little influence in the previous analysis, I did not include it here (remember, the influence of context by tradition was statistically insignificant for both stem-cell research and abortion and, though it was statistically significant for homosexual marriage, its overall explanatory power was very weak).

Table 4.6

Political Tolerance Factorial ANOVA Design (Context by Issue Attitude)

Issue Attitude	*Predictor Variables*	*Sum of Squares*	*F*	*Significance*	*Eta-squared*
Abortion	Context	2.056	.054	.948	.000
	Abortion Attitude	128.721	1.686	.155	.030
	Context-by-Abortion	152.400	.998	.439	.036
Total Sum of Squares = 4241.977; F = 1.232; Significance = .254; Eta-Squared = .078					
Stem Cell Research	Context	.902	.023	.977	.000
	Stem Cell Attitude	128.76	1.647	.164	.030
	Context-by-Stem Cell Research	93.822	.600	.777	.022
Total Sum of Squares = 4241.977; F = .864; Significance = .599; Eta-Squared = .056					
Homosexual Marriage	Context	7.22	.182	.833	.002
	Homosexual Marriage	56.48	.713	.584	.013
	Context-by-Homosexual Marriage	115.37	.728	.666	.027
Total Sum of Squares = 4241.977; F = .663; Significance = .809; Eta-Squared = .043					

As can be seen from a review of table 4.6, there is no statistically significant model in which political tolerance is influenced by either a specific issue attitude or the interaction of context and issue attitude. Furthermore, none of the predictor variables within the model is statistically significant. In short, each equation (or model) as a whole is insignificant; and within each equation, the predictor variables are also insignificant. Furthermore, the explanatory power of each model and for the predictor variables in each of those models is low to nonexistent.[15] I conduct one more analysis, in an attempt to improve the explanatory power of issue attitude on political tolerance.

This next analysis involves creating a cumulative scale of "opposition" by combining the scores related to all three issue attitudes of abortion, stem-cell research, and homosexual marriage (remember, each question asked about opposition toward the particular issue, as can be seen in table 4.1). Based on that cumulative scale, I create a high/middle/low variable in which subjects are coded as high (e.g., high level of opposition to abortion, stem-cell research, and homosexual marriage), low (e.g., low level of opposition to abortion, stem-cell research, and homosexual marriage), and middle (e.g., centrist) based on each respondent's cumulative score. With three issue-attitude questions, the cumulative issue-attitude "opposition" scale ranges from 3 to 15 in which a 3 corresponds to a high level of opposition and a 15 corresponds to a low level of opposition.

Table 4.7

Political Tolerance Factorial ANOVA Design (Context by Level of Opposition)

Political Tolerance	*Predictor Variables*	*Sum of Squares*	*F*	*Significance*	*Eta-Squared*
	Context	3.641	.093	.912	.000
	Level of Opposition	11.643	.296	.744	.002
	Context-by-Opposition	61.981	.789	.534	.015
Total Sum of Squares = 4241.977; F = .608; Significance = .771; Eta-Squared = .023					

To create the high/middle/low categories, I wanted to compare those who strongly agreed with opposition toward these issues with those who strongly disagreed with opposition toward these issues. Therefore, I coded 3 to 6 as "high opposition"; 12 to 15 as "low opposition"; and 7 to 11 as "centrist." As can be seen from table 4.7, once again, issue attitude (e.g., high/middle/low level of opposition) fails to exhibit any explanatory power as it relates to political tolerance. The model as a whole is statistically insignificant with an F statistic of .608 (significance .771), and the eta squared is inconsequential at approximately 2 percent. Furthermore, all of the individual predictor variables were statistically insignificant while exhibiting virtually no explanatory power as evidenced by the eta-squared values.[16]

Summary

The central goal of this particular chapter was to begin to discuss the relationship between issue-attitude position and political tolerance. Often, those who hold the most conservative views on issues such as abortion, stem-cell research, and homosexual marriage are deemed politically intolerant because of these views. This perception is exacerbated when those with conservative views base their attitude positions on their religion. This is the case even though a widely accepted definition of political tolerance, a definition used throughout this research, has nothing to do with issue-attitude position. Given this, I wanted to accentuate a moral versus social opposition to abortion, stem-cell research, and homosexual marriage and test for the potential linkage between a moral opposition, versus a social or neutral opposition, with political tolerance. The totality of the results from this chapter, while (weakly) reaffirming the link between religious tradition and religious commitment and issue-attitude position, suggests that this relationship between religion and issue-attitude position does not translate into an influence on political tolerance. Consistent with chapters 2 and 3, this chapter continues to suggest that the influence of religion on political tolerance is minimal to nonexistent—or at least is not as detrimental as popular perceptions have implied and several previous studies have indicated. Furthermore, it suggests that issue-attitude positions, even when informed by religion (either religious belonging or religious commitment), do not *ipso facto* translate into less (or a lack of) political tolerance.

As stated at the outset of the chapter, I consider this data to be exploratory in nature. There are, undoubtedly, several issues one can raise with the data and the study here. For example, was a survey-based experiment an appropriate means of studying this topic? Were the distinctions between social, neutral, and moral contexts appropriate? If they were appropriate, could the questions asked in each context have been written differently? For example, as an experiment, the question wording was the manipulation of the predictor variable; therefore, it is fair to ask whether the manipulation was strong enough. Despite the critiques that can be made of the data and design of this particular chapter, it is clearly an adequate design that resulted in data and results supported by previous research (affirming a link between religion and issue attitudes) and by the data and results from previous chapters in this book (as is the case with the continued findings suggesting that a fatally detrimental relationship between religion and political tolerance does not exist). In the final chapter of this book, I will discuss the implications of the results presented throughout this book as they relate to religion, political tolerance, and liberal democracy.

Chapter 5

Political *In*tolerance

Is It Really not about Religion?

If there is no real truth, there is no reason for me to be tolerant. Without some kind of beliefs which cause me to value you as a person, even though I disagree with you, why should I be tolerant toward you? If you are getting in my way, why shouldn't I walk over you, if I have the power to do so? . . . . If there is no real truth, we cannot place any limits on tolerance. If society is to be able to function, we need some shared beliefs that will move us to value other people as people, even when they disagree with us, but which will also enable us to put limits on our individual freedom of choice, for the good of society as a whole.

—*David Couchman*

I began this book with the simple premise that religion, at least in contemporary America, is not the threat to liberal democracy that it is generally purported to be by the mass media and academia. By approaching this topic as a political question from the perspective of a trained political scientist and placing this study within the broader political science literature that addresses political tolerance as well as the literature from the religion and politics subfield of political science, I examined the relationship between religion and political tolerance within a liberal democracy using quantitative, qualitative, and experimental techniques. The specific purpose of chapter 2 was to reexamine the link between religion and political tolerance in a comprehensive quantitative analysis that brought together the mainstream political tolerance literature that had developed a "least-liked" measure for political tolerance and demonstrated the importance of psychological and political predictors of political tolerance with the religion and politics literature that had established the multidimensional nature of religion (e.g., belief, belonging, and behavior), as well as the best means of measuring or capturing those dimensions.

Contrary to prevailing orthodoxy and numerous research studies stretching back several decades, the results derived in that chapter demonstrated the lack of a detrimental influence of religion on political tolerance. First, increased religious commitment did not directly lead to decreased levels of political tolerance, and doctrinal orthodoxy did not directly lead to decreased political tolerance. The negative relationship between religious commitment and doctrinal orthodoxy to political tolerance were both indirect in nature, and the substantive effects were extremely small. Finally, the influence of education on religious commitment was such that increased education leads to more—not less—religious commitment, which was also contrary to expectations derived from theory (and previous results) in various social science sources.

Thus, in contradistinction to an axiomatic assumption within the discipline of political science (and possibly within academia in the aggregate) that religion is incompatible with political tolerance, the results of chapter 2 tell a different story. This different story was reinforced and added to in chapter 3 with the information culled from the qualitative data obtained by using focus groups. The results from the focus group chapter demonstrate—through the words and perspectives culled from direct communication with the religiously inclined—that these citizens value and support liberal democracy. No one within any of the focus groups was at odds with the traditions of a liberal democracy, which presupposes conditions for competition of ideas—even ideas with which they disagree—in the political marketplace. I argued in chapter 3 that the focus group participants (across all four religious traditions) recognize that disagreements, which sometimes can be very difficult and contentious, do exist and that some means of handling them must be maintained. This speaks directly to the issue of political tolerance.

Although the focus group participants clearly expressed the idea that the religious clauses of the First Amendment (in an aggregate assessment of the participants' input) did not mean that —at the time of our nation's founding—there existed or exists today an absolute and impregnable wall of separation; nonetheless, these same focus group participants did not in any manner indicate that religious authority should have dominion over our secular governmental authority in a formal institutionalized manner. This is important because it speaks directly to the democratic socialization of our citizens—even the religiously inclined ones—to recognize that our formal governmental structures are not to be an official arm of any religious authority. The importance of this is that it demonstrates that the members of these four different focus group, each group members of a particular congregation, have been socialized into an acceptance of and preference for a liberal democratic form of government and not a government beholden to a particular religious authority, which is just what Kraynak (2001) argues.

In short, the participants clearly understood the difference between separation of church and state versus an inclusive relationship between religion and politics. For the participants across all four focus groups, the role of faith in civic society was, predominantly, an individual role. That is, all the focus groups suggested that the dominant means of faith influencing civic society was for individuals of faith to take their faith and values into the political marketplace, permitting their individual behavior in civic society to be the conduit of how faith and civic society interconnected. This speaks to an acceptance of and appreciation for the give-and-take of a liberal democratic system in which some individuals will base their participation and policy beliefs on faith-based values, while others are equally permitted not to do so. These individuals view themselves as legitimate participants in the process of liberal democratic decision-making. The religious individuals among us are, in the aggregate, not against liberal democracy; they grapple with issues of political tolerance (frequently more intensely than the nonreligious). Far from expressing a desire to eliminate other views from the marketplace of ideas, they instead focus on participating in civil society in which they can represent their views vis-à-vis others whom they fully expect and accept will be in that marketplace with them. This is consistent with the Christian theology that argues for the individual's responsibility in society for his or her actions as a manifestation of the Christian conceptualization of the individual human's responsibility before Christ.

Once the relationship between religion, political tolerance, and liberal democracy was examined from both a quantitative and qualitative framework in chapter 3, the next chapter turned to an experimental design to study the relationship between religion, political tolerance, and public opinion within a liberal democracy. The central goal of this chapter was to begin to discuss the relationship between issue-attitude position and political tolerance. As discussed, those who hold the most conservative views on issues such as abortion, stem-cell research, and homosexual marriage are perceived as politically intolerant because they simply hold these views. This perception is exacerbated when those with conservative views base their attitude positions on their religion. The totality of the conclusions from chapter 4 was that the established relationship between religion and issue-attitude position does not translate into any influence (negative, positive, or otherwise) on political tolerance. More specifically, it suggests that issue attitude positions, even when informed by religion (either religious belonging or religious commitment), do not *ipso facto* translate into less (or a lack of) political tolerance on the part of the actor. This has been argued throughout this book, and it is certainly central to my thesis because it speaks to, reconfirms, and highlights the very meaning of political tolerance in a liberal democracy. This is the opposite of the common definition of political tolerance as consisting of a certain acceptance or concurrence with preapproved issue-attitude positions.

But, in many ways, this link between what is considered conservative issue attitudes and political tolerance is the hardest to neutralize academically or within mainstream culture. This is because of the overwhelming presumption that attitudes of a traditional/religious nature concerning issues such as abortion and homosexuality are, on their very face, intolerant, and therefore represent a detrimental or fatal influence to our most basic rights and liberties. The results from chapter 4 demonstrate that this presumption has no empirical support. What is not addressed in this book—or anywhere else extensively—is that on some of the most contentious issues, such as abortion, many religiously inclined individuals have neither accepted nor may ever accept that these are "rights," let alone a basic civil right having the same status as speech, petition, and assembly. What I am suggesting is that although speech, petition, and assembly are firmly rooted as basic civil rights in the lexicon of American culture and liberal democracy, rights regarding abortion (and homosexuality) have not achieved such a status (for good, bad, or otherwise). When they do achieve such status, the contentiousness over these issues may very well cease. It is also fair to point out that the acceptance or rejection of these issues as basic or natural rights is not limited to the religious community. Many individuals in liberal democracies who view themselves as secular still reject the idea of expanding rights beyond the basic ones recognized by a liberal democracy.

Nevertheless, as a society, we must be cognizant of the fact that many religiously inclined individuals rely on their faith values to inform what are inherently public policy issue attitudes. Therefore, they may not (perhaps may never) accept issues such as abortion as a "right" that Americans should not be denied. Inherently, these sources of values cannot be distinguished from the value sources of secular individuals. Consistent with the rationale of Martin Luther King Jr., articulated in his "Letter from Birmingham Jail," there may ever be a contingent of Americans who truly believe that "a just law is a man-made code that squares with the moral law or the law of God. An unjust law is a code that is out of harmony with the moral law. To put it in terms of St. Thomas Aquinas: An unjust law is a law that is not rooted in eternal law or natural law" (King Jr. 1964, 82). A discussion of moral law and the law of God is far beyond the purview of this book, but the central point remains—that political tolerance is not about attitudes toward a specific set of issues. The data from chapter 4 reinforce this empirically. Furthermore, abortion and homosexual rights, being products of the twentieth century, have not yet run their course within American politics.

Discussion

A new realization emerges then that if one wants to understand political intolerance, Christianity in contemporary America is not the place to either look or to place blame. Rather than being an impediment to liberal democratic ideals, Christians across numerous religious traditions participate freely in and reinforce liberal democratic politics and fully expect, realize, and accept that others—even those who disagree with them—will do the same. Political tolerance, taken together, is not influenced by religious belief, religious commitment, or religious tradition. In addition, conservative, even religiously influenced, issue-attitude positions have absolutely no influence on political tolerance. Clearly, then, the religiously inclined are socialized to support democratic values and openness to diverse opinions. American culture permeates the secular and the religious in such a way that democratic values and an acceptance of diversity (particularly of opinion) is the norm and not the exception. In summary, religion is not linked to political intolerance, and liberal democracy is not threatened by Christian adherents.

Nevertheless, I hold no illusion about the reception that these findings will illicit. Expectedly, most academics, particularly within the liberal arts and social sciences, will find it utterly incomprehensible that anything good can come from religion. Ergo, these findings and indeed the research itself, must be either wrong or biased. Perhaps their "bias" is toward the notion of the Judeo-Christian tradition of a personal God, as opposed to the concept of an impersonal transcendental deity. Finally, the liberal-leaning mainstream Christian religionists, such as the liberal protestant sects, will certainly concur that they are certainly not a problem to either political tolerance or liberal democracy, but surely (they'll say) those coreligionists that are part of the Christian right cannot be tolerant or accepting of liberal democracy. Something, for certain, from their perspective in what was analyzed and discussed in this work will be found lacking or wrong. The problem, it seems to me, is that there are three types of biases working against a reconsideration of religion in contemporary America, its specific relationship to political tolerance, its general relationship to liberal democracy, and the notion that religious individuals—particularly evangelical Christians—are no more or no less a threat than any other committed Christian, liberal or otherwise. Those biases can be construed as a sectarian bias, a rationality/reason bias, and a psychological bias.

Sectarian Bias

American and European inquiry into religion and religious faith is biased in favor of secular truth. Even when examined, it is studied without sympathy and understanding. It is the only area of "ethnic" study where the investigator is found to be acceptable even though he or she may completely reject or even ridicule adherents and their subject matter. It is as though a racist was found acceptable to study race. The latter would be found completely nonsensical and unacceptable, yet the former is common practice. In short, this is the secular bias.

According to Rodney Stark ([1996] 1997, 209), theology is deemed irrelevant in the study of history today. He argues: "Historians today are more than willing to discuss how social factors shaped religious doctrines. Unfortunately, at the same time they have become somewhat reluctant to discuss how doctrines may have shaped social factors." In studying the reasons and factors that contributed to the rise of Christianity in the Western world, Stark says, "[s]urely doctrine was central to nursing the sick during times of plague, to the rejection of abortion and infanticide, to fertility, and to organizational vigor." In general, the picture we get from Stark ([1996] 1997, 209; including 2003 and 2005) is that, historically, the effects of Christianity have produced many good consequences that eventually resulted in a Western civilization that, among other things, provided its citizens with greater freedoms and a better standard of living than non-Western civilizations. These positive consequences include the abolition of slavery both in Old World Europe and again in the "new" world of the Americas. The Judeo-Christian tradition brought the rise of science in Christian Europe and the commitment to reason among Christian theologians. That commitment to reason enabled the rise of science to occur; and this same commitment to reason among Christian theologians led to freedom, capitalism, and Western success, especially in development of liberal democracy. Of course, Stark is familiar with and does not ignore the negative consequences of how religion and ideas about God (particularly a monotheistic God) affected the West and Western civilization, but he does put them into context. In contemporary America, it is difficult to find someone with Stark's academic rigor and intellect in a forceful and compelling manner articulating the benefits of theology, doctrine, religion, and ideas of God. Most of what is articulated on these topics today has a distinct focus on the negative with a presumption that little to nothing of value can accrue from faith—particularly when it is a faith that advocates the "wrong" set of issue-attitude opinions.

In contemporary America, any religious doctrine that contravenes the modern orthodoxy is not only deemed intolerant but often is presumed to be fatal to liberal democracy. One of many examples of this is a quote from the 2006 bestselling book *American Fascists: The Christian Right and the War on America*. The author, Chris Hedges (2006, 21) writes: "But within this mass of divergent, fractious and varied groups [of evangelicals] is this core group of powerful Christian dominionists who have latched on to the despair, isolation, disconnectedness and fear that drives many people into these churches."[1] You would never suspect that, according to polls and data from the Pew Research Center for the People & the Press, those who attend religious services weekly or more often are happier than those attending less often and that those who seldom or never attend services are the least likely to say they are very happy. The same is true when income is added to the equation. For those in similar income categories, individuals who indicate that they attend church regularly report higher levels of happiness than those who do not.[2]

Hedges, who grew up Presbyterian with a minister as a father, is of course, objective, if for no other reason than his argument is wrapped in the commitment to liberal democracy, and his treatise against the Christian right, comes from an individual "steeped" in Christian tradition and the Bible. Hedges relates his father's commitment to the "gay-rights movement," opposition to the Vietnam War, and his early support for Martin Luther King Jr. and the Civil Rights movement. Thus, within the first several pages, readers clearly understand that Hedges is on the "liberal" or "non-detrimental" side of religion. His religious belief comports with current mainstream liberal protestant orthodoxy as it relates to issue-attitude positions on abortion, war, homosexual rights, and so on. However, of those with a different set of issue-attitude positions (that are also based on their Christian faith), he writes an entire polemic about the perceived evils of their issue-attitude positions and the supposed ill intent of Christians who have as their specific objective the end of liberal democracy as true Americans know it. That is the reason for the "American Fascists" in the title.

Varied statements from the book's first chapter represent the standard fare for those in contemporary America (and Europe) who view evangelical Christians (e.g., the Christian Right) as "the" enemy within. He says, "[t]here is enough hatred, bigotry, and lust for violence in the pages of the Bible to satisfy anyone bent on justifying cruelty and violence. . . . And the Bible has long been used in the wrong hands—such as antebellum slave owners in the American South who quoted from it to defend slavery . . ." (Hedges 2006, 5). Of course, Chris Hedges—unlike a Rodney Stark—does not appear willing or able to put the positive and negative consequences of religion into a broader historical context. Completely absent from his comment is the contemporaneous recognition that the Abolition movement was spearheaded by Christians in America (e.g., the Quakers) and, a century earlier, in Old World Europe, particularly England (Stark 2003, chap. 4). *American Fascists* tells us "[a]lthough the values of capitalism are antithetical to Christ's vision . . . . the gospel of prosperity . . . has formulated a belief system that delights corporate America" (Hedges 2006, 22). Again, Hedges is wrong on his facts—it was Christianity that enabled capitalism. From Stark, we read:

> Just as have the other world religions, for centuries Christianity proclaimed the moral and spiritual superiority of asceticism and expressed antagonism toward commerce and finance. But these teachings were resoundingly rejected in the twelfth and thirteenth centuries by Catholic theologians who stoutly defended private property and the pursuit of profits. How could this have occurred? Because as new commercial activities began in the great monastic estates, their moral status was reassessed by theologians who concluded that previous prohibitions had been based on an inadequate theology (Stark 2005, xv).

Hedges states that:

> It is perhaps telling that our closest allies in the United Nations on issues dealing with reproductive rights, one of the few issues where we cooperate with other nations, are Islamic states such as Iran. But then the Christian Right and radical Islamists, although locked in a holy war, increasingly mirror each other. They share the same obsessions. They do not tolerate other forms of belief or disbelief. They are at war with artistic and cultural expression. They seek to silence the media. They call for the subjugation of women. They promote severe sexual repression, and they seek to express themselves through violence (Hedges 2006, 24).

There is just no support for this view of evangelical Christians and the Christian Right, taken together, in contemporary America. And equating the "Christian Right" with "radical Islamists" is, at best, intellectually disingenuous, at worst, wholly prejudiced. For example, liberal democracy exists in many nations that have a historical Christian influence and culture, yet not one currently exists in an Islamic country. The specific historical conditions that are difficult to ignore is that negative human behavior has existed everywhere on the globe historically. Only in countries and continents influenced predominantly by the Judeo-Christian tradition has science, economic advancement, technology, and, finally, liberal democracy been established for any long-term duration.

One would not be as troubled about these types of misrepresentations, with empirical evidence to the contrary, except for the fact that—as an example of a majority perception—what Hedges writes is considered the "truth" in mainstream culture as well as academic circles. The socialization of this perspective is so universal that what Hedges presents sounds correct at first glance. However, in actuality it is not.

> Between one picture of religious believers as resident aliens and another as hostile to liberal values there is not much to choose. Fortunately, both pictures are inaccurate ones . . . . One can, of course, always find some religious believers in the United States who reject liberal society in favor of apocalyptic beliefs. But they are a small minority, and a shrinking one at that . . . . Despite the attention they receive, religious extremists are often difficult to find in the United States (Wolfe 2003, 253–54).

Sadly, the specific type of sectarian bias promoted and advanced by Hedges and others has captured the imaginations and minds of many so that they place evangelical Christians (as the Christian Right) on a morally equivalent plane as militant, radical Islamists—all the while ignoring obvious differences and research and evidence to the contrary. Then, by many, this stereotype is transferred to the Christian religion in general so that the perception of religion as the root of political intolerance, when empirically it is not, continues to be promulgated as truth.

Reason or Rationality Bias

Another bias that impedes a reconsideration of the relationship between religion, political tolerance, and liberal democracy within contemporary America is the bias of reason or rationality. "Thus, until recently, the social scientific study of religion was nothing of the sort. The field was far more concerned with discrediting religion than with understanding it. This is clear when it is realized that only in the area of religious belief and behavior have social scientists not based their theories on a rational choice premise" (Stark [1996] 1997, 166; italics from original). Although "[s]ocial scientists have begun to explain religious activity as a product of individual choices made by rational people" (Wolfe 2003, 246), a long line of scholars, as well as mainstream commentators, continues to promote (implicitly or explicitly) the irrationality of religious belief and activity (Stark [1996] 1997, 166).

Once again, to demonstrate this point regarding a bias of irrationality toward religion and religious individuals, Hedges' 2006 bestseller is illustrative because his view represents a mainstream presentation of the irrationality of religious choice. He says that radical "dominionists" are manipulating millions to embrace "a world of miracles and signs and removes followers from a rational, reality-based world. . . . These believers have abandoned . . . their trust and belief in the world of science, law, and rationality" (Hedges 2006, 35). The assumption here is that if one accepts miracles and signs then one could not believe in science, law, or rationality. Those who believe that religion lacks any component at all of rationality are simply wrong. Wolfe (2003, 246) argues that regarding the use of rational choice theory in the explanation of religion or religious behavior, "the only issue worth discussing with respect to rational-choice theory is not whether it ought to be utilized but how much it actually explains." Furthermore, Stark (2003, chap. 8) spends considerable time explaining the rationality of religion—and he does so quite convincingly.

Nonetheless, Jerolmack and Porpora (2004) argue against any role for rational choice theory in understanding religion and religious motives. They specifically challenge the rational choice theory of religion presented by Rodney Stark and Roger Finke (Stark 1999; Stark & Finke 2000) in their groundbreaking works. In speaking of this theory, they argue that "it is only rational choice theory's own, restrictive definition of rationality that renders altruism irrational" (Jerolmack & Porpora 2004, 148). Consequently, they attempt to develop a multiple theory of reason that would include all possible actions. So in addition to instrumental reason (rational choice), they have added normative rationality and epistemic rationality. Their problem is that they do not understand, or refuse to accept, the question that Stark and Finke are addressing.

The problem as specified by Stark and Finke is that social scientists, particularly sociologists, refuse to ascribe rationality to religious acts that is on a level plane with other human endeavors. Stark and Finke argue that uniquely, religion in academia, even when it is studied, is relegated to some type of irrational act, akin to witchcraft or seeing ghosts. Social scientists' own bias against religion does not generally permit them to ascribe rationality when theorizing about religion. Jerolmack and Porpora (2004, 157) recognize this issue when they conclude "[w]e share the belief that religious commitment is a rational choice as opposed to a choice that is irrational or even nonrational." This is precisely Stark and Finke's point. Religion is so foreign a subject that it is inherently denied rationality by the very fact that rational choice theory is rarely, if ever, applied to this particular human act; but it is used to understand most other human activity. By this willingness to ascribe rational choice theory to other acts but not religious acts leaves religion to be viewed as inherently irrational.

Although Stark and Finke may very well accept other theories of religion as being viable, their point is that religion is not given the respect of reason by social scientists. For social scientists in the twenty-first century, rational choice theory is scientific reason. What Jerolmack and Porpora do is take that quality away from reason again by adding other philosophical reasons that social scientists do not recognize. When they "reclaim from rational choice theory the normative dimension of religion and especially of religious commitment" (2004, 158), they place religion, for social scientists, in a unique place not inhabited by any other human activity. One of the problems with this new habitat is that it is not open for inquiry, by social scientists, to other human activity; and therefore, always remains in the metaphysical or irrational plane. Metaphysics and irrationality frequently have been presented as in opposition to the enlightenment democratic ideals.

Psychological Bias

If individuals can be manipulated to make an irrational decision regarding religion, the real questions becomes how and why. One explanation comes from social psychology that began with the work of Adorno, Frenkel-Brunswick, Levinson, and Sanford (1950). The problem was one of personality disorder. According to Adorno and the other authors, one of the primary personality disorders was an authoritarian personality; those individuals with an authoritarian personality are likely to be attracted to groups with strong leaders expressing a strong opposition—and possibly hate—toward "outgroups." Another related explanation is found within sociology in which alienation and isolation lead one to become associated with conservative evangelical Christian organizations. The argument is that the "religious right" has benefited from the isolationism, a lack of attachment to extended family (as well as to community and social organizations) as a result of contemporary life. Thus, the Christian Right (e.g., evangelicals) benefits because there are so many ungrounded and isolated individuals who are attracted by offers of a connection to others and to a larger community (Wilcox & Larson 2006). Conover and Gray (1981, 4) argue, "Without such organizational involvement in their lives, people are thought to grow restless and alienated. . . . Such individuals are 'easy prey' for right-wing movements." When Hedges (2006, 201) writes that it is "despair, isolation, disconnectedness and fear that drives many people into these churches," his portrayal is but a mainstream presentation of what is, essentially, a scholarly argument (from within sociology). Whether the problem is a personality disorder or societal alienation, religion is a type of "crutch" that is needed by the unstable or the ungrounded (and in both cases, religious choice is by definition, therefore, irrational). It is extremely difficult to overcome the perception that only the weak or those with some type of personality or societal problem would choose religious belief or activity, even among educated citizens, as attested to by Wolfe (2003, 249) when he says, "Somehow the news about the transformation of religion has not been transmitted, at least to a significant number of intellectuals who write about the subject." Hence, reconsidering the relationship between contemporary Christianity in the United States in relationship to political tolerance in particular and liberal democracy in general, continues to require persistence.

Christianity and Democracy

Liberal democracy owes its existence to the Judeo-Christian tradition. Accurately, pagan Athens recognized that humans are political animals; but at least a millennia before, it was Judeo-Christian ideas in the book of Genesis that gave rise to the belief that each human was a unique individual. To this day, that concept is most dominant in countries within the Judeo-Christian tradition. In addition, the greatest influence of individualism is in those societies that have been dominated by Anglo-Saxon Protestantism; they have recognized an exclusive personal relationship between the individual and God. That idea of the individual is the singular preeminent presupposition of a liberal democracy. This was the very basis of John Locke's and subsequently Thomas Jefferson's conceptualization of individuals' inalienable rights endowed by their Creator, not the government. Continuously ignored has been that assumption of the individual and its religious source.

I have attempted to bring to light in this book, empirically, what Locke knew theoretically—that the Christian religion is necessary for the idea of a liberal democracy. As a whole, Christian believers tend to support the principles of liberal democratic governance. In all the studies presented here, this has held true among all the religious groups and individuals discussed. Political intolerance, which is anathema to liberal democracy, is not the purview of the religious. What is true is that many secular individuals, and possibly some religious ones, have been socialized to presume that this is the case. Empirically, as has been shown, there is no evidence to support this within the American Judeo-Christian tradition. Books such as *American Fascists* and the general framework of belief of secular Western intellectuals is so encompassing that even history has to change to accommodate the truth about liberal democracy.

Even such works as *The Blackwell Companion to Political Theology* find it necessary to argue that the root of liberal democracy is the French Revolution and not the American Revolution. Although this is a work about religion and religiosity, it would seem to be so repugnant to argue that Christianity gave rise to liberal democracy that the root has to be a revolution whose very goal was anticlerical and antireligious. That is factually wrong; but credit cannot go to Christianity. "But democracy as we know it developed only after the European Enlightenment and *especially* the French Revolution. As a result it has become the polity of modernity" (de Gruchy 2004, 441; italics added). The French Revolution was irrelevant to the notion of a liberal democracy; it was out of the American Revolution that a liberal democracy was implemented, and its ideals were taken directly from John Locke of England, a devout Christian. The American experiment preceded the French one and remains a success; the French experiment was derived from the American one and is best known for its fall into tyranny. For a work on political theology, its uniqueness is the insistence by Europeans not to give credit, even when studying the subject of religion, for the positive aspects of liberal democracy. The French Revolution failed because it was not a religious-based revolution; but, rather an antireligious one.

The success of America as a liberal democracy, so far one of the few, is credited to its ongoing religious underpinning. It maintained the Judeo-Christian tradition encapsulated in the Anglo-Saxon protestant movements of the unique individual who had individual responsibility. It is the idea of the unique individual that led political thinkers, such as Locke and Jefferson, to approach the idea of political tolerance as a necessary condition for political democracy. Without that religious idea of the individual how can one make sense of the need for a liberal democracy? What this book has shown empirically is that religiosity continuous to be supportive of liberal democracy. Liberal democracy, many authorities have argued, presupposes political tolerance. Although many modern writers have argued for a variety of reasons that religion is anathema to political tolerance, empirically we have shown that in the American context, that is just not the case.

Three general biases give rise to a negative perception of the relationship between religion and liberal democracy: sectarian or secular bias, rational bias, and psychological bias. These have held sway for much of the twentieth century out of a certain socialized norm rather than from empirical findings. This work has shown that these biases are not supported empirically as a problem for religiosity when confronted with political tolerance. In fact not only is religion/religiosity not a factor in political tolerance; historically, religion and religiosity have been the very foundation of political tolerance. The interesting question is "Can the nonreligious be as supportive of political tolerance as to make a liberal democracy possible with the religious Christian citizens?

Final Thoughts

Recently, I was presented with the opportunity to read Russell Kirk's *The American Cause*. I was not familiar with his work or its conceptualization of the relationship between the religiosity of the founding fathers and American principles of a liberal democracy. In this brief work, Kirk argues that three principles control any people: a set of moral convictions, political convictions, and economic convictions. In setting out the moral ideas and convictions that govern American life, Kirk argues that the United States of America is a Christian nation. It should be clarified that he did not specify that one had to be a Christian; in fact, quite the opposite. He argues ([1957] 2002, 30) that "Christian concepts of natural law, natural rights, and necessary limitations to human ambitions all govern our politics and even our economic system. That all Americans do not always abide by Christian teachings scarcely needs to be confessed." At one point, Kirk states of America's founders: "Not one of our early statesman was a professed atheist; and all of our presidents, with the possible exception of Jefferson, have publicly professed faith in Christian doctrines, (Jefferson drew up privately his own version of what he believed to be the direct teachings of Christ, the 'Jefferson Bible'; and though unconvinced of the divinity of Jesus, he was profoundly attached to Christian morals" ([1957] 2002, 36). Thinking about Kirk's work and our current questions about the exportability of liberal democracy, I was struck by the stark difference between Kirk's presentation of the role of Christian moral convictions, including how they influenced American life and society (particularly as this role relates to our nation's founding), and how contemporary commentators present the role and influence of Christian moral convictions in today's America. How is it that, in the overwhelming aggregate, a group of Christians, with (arguably) a Christian worldview, managed to construct and sustain our liberal democracy; yet, today it is the very Christians who so many educated citizens among us believe are threatening liberal democracy? The studies in this book have shown that this perception of religiosity, generally, and Christianity, specifically, is a pure flight of fancy and has no grounding in the factual evidence.

Appendices

Appendix A

Survey

Hello, my name is ____________, and I am calling from the ______________ Public Opinion Laboratory. I am conducting a study for a Purdue University instructor regarding certain groups in society, some current issues, and your beliefs about religion. This interview is completely voluntary and confidential. This survey takes less than 15 minutes to complete.

Q1. In the United States today, do you think that terrorists are a big threat, a moderate threat, or no threat to Americans?

1. A big threat
2. A moderate threat
3. No threat at all
4. Don't know
5. No answer

Q2. Now I would like to ask you about some different groups you may have heard of. Please tell me which group you like the least from this list: socialists, the Ku Klux Klan, pro-choice people, and pro-life people.

1. Socialists
2. the Ku Klux Klan
3. Pro-choice people
4. Pro-life people
5. Not ascertained/Refused to answer

Q3. Next, I'm going to read the names of four more groups. Tell me which group you like the least from this list.

1. Atheists
2. Homosexuals
3. Religious Fundamentalists
4. Feminists
5. Not Ascertained/Refused to answer

Q4. Taking the two groups you just mentioned—(*Insert Q2 answer*) and (*Insert Q3 answer*)—, which of these two groups do you like the least?

1. Socialists
2. the Ku Klux Klan
3. Pro-choice people
4. Pro-life people
5. Atheists
6. Homosexuals
7. Religious fundamentalists
8. Feminists
9. Not ascertained/Refused to answer

Q5. Other than terrorists or Iraqis, is there any other group that I did not mention that you like less than (*Insert Q4 answer*), the one you just selected?

If NO, code the group from Q4:

1. Socialists
2. the Ku Klux Klan
3. Pro-choice people
4. Pro-life people
5. Atheists
6. Homosexuals
7. Religious fundamentalists
8. Feminists

If YES, record the answer given verbatim:

1. Other group: (Please specify) *RECORD VERBATIM*

   ____

2. I do not like any of them/Can't decide (*DO NOT READ*)

   ____

3. Don't know (*DO NOT READ*)

   ____

4. No answer/Refused to answer (*DO NOT READ*)

   ____

Q6. I am going to read you a list of statements about (*Insert Q5 answer*). For each statement, indicate whether you agree or disagree and how strongly you feel about that.

STATEMENTS

a. (Members of the/The) (*Insert Q5 answer*) should be banned from running for public office in the United States. Do you agree or disagree? Do you feel strongly or not so strongly about that?

- ❑ Strongly Agree
- ❑ Agree
- ❑ Disagree
- ❑ Strongly Disagree
- ❑ Don't Know
- ❑ Refused to Answer
- ❑ No Answer

b. (Members of the/The) (*Insert Q5 answer*) should be allowed to teach in public schools, Do you agree or disagree? Do you feel strongly or not so strongly about that?

- ❑ Strongly Agree
- ❑ Agree
- ❑ Disagree
- ❑ Strongly Disagree
- ❑ Don't Know
- ❑ Refused to Answer
- ❑ No Answer

c. (Members of the/The) (*Insert Q5 answer*) should be outlawed. *READ AS NECESSARY:* Do you agree or disagree? Do you feel strongly or not so strongly about that?

- ❑ Strongly Agree
- ❑ Agree
- ❑ Disagree
- ❑ Strongly Disagree
- ❑ Don't Know
- ❑ Refused to Answer
- ❑ No Answer

d. (Members of the/The) (*Insert Q5 answer*) should be allowed to make a public speech. READ AS NECESSARY: Do you agree or disagree? Do you feel strongly or not so strongly about that?

- ❑ Strongly Agree
- ❑ Agree
- ❑ Disagree
- ❑ Strongly Disagree
- ❑ Don't Know
- ❑ Refused to Answer
- ❑ No Answer

e. (Members of the/The) (*Insert Q5 answer*) should be allowed to hold public rallies. *READ AS NECESSARY:* Do you agree or disagree? Do you feel strongly or not so strongly about that?

- ❑ Strongly Agree
- ❑ Agree
- ❑ Disagree
- ❑ Strongly Disagree
- ❑ Don't Know
- ❑ Refused to Answer
- ❑ No Answer

Q7. Thinking about (the) (*Insert Q5 answer*), would you describe (the) (*Insert Q5 answer*) as safe or dangerous?
IF SAFE: Is that very safe or only somewhat safe?
IF DANGEROUS: Is that very dangerous or only somewhat dangerous?

1. Very safe
2. Somewhat safe
3. Somewhat dangerous
4. Very dangerous
5. Don't know (DO NOT READ)
6. No answer/Refused to answer (DO NOT READ)

Q8. Now I am going to read some statements some people might use to describe their general opinions about things. For each statement, tell me whether you agree or disagree and how strongly you feel about that.

STATEMENTS

a. There are two kinds of people in this world: those who are for the truth and those who are against the truth. Do you agree or disagree? Do you feel strongly or not so strongly about that?

- ☐ Strongly Agree
- ☐ Agree
- ☐ Disagree
- ☐ Strongly Disagree
- ☐ Don't Know
- ☐ Refused to Answer
- ☐ No Answer

b. Most of the ideas which get printed nowadays aren't worth the paper they are printed on. *READ AS NECESSARY:* Do you agree or disagree? Do you feel strongly or not so strongly about that?

- ☐ Strongly Agree
- ☐ Agree
- ☐ Disagree
- ☐ Strongly Disagree
- ☐ Don't Know
- ☐ Refused to Answer
- ☐ No Answer

c. No matter what a person's political beliefs are, he is entitled to the same legal rights and protections as anyone else. *READ AS NECESSARY:* Do you agree or disagree? Do you feel strongly or not so strongly about that?

- ☐ Strongly Agree
- ☐ Agree
- ☐ Disagree
- ☐ Strongly Disagree
- ☐ Don't Know
- ☐ Refused to Answer
- ☐ No Answer

d. I believe in free speech for all, no matter what their views might be. *READ AS NECESSARY:* Do you agree or disagree? Do you feel strongly or not so strongly about that?

- ☐ Strongly Agree
- ☐ Agree
- ☐ Disagree
- ☐ Strongly Disagree
- ☐ Don't Know
- ☐ Refused to Answer
- ☐ No Answer

Q9. Next, I am going to read some statements some people might use to describe their general opinions about themselves. For each statement, tell me whether the statement is true or false about you.

STATEMENTS

a. I am certainly lacking in self-confidence. Is this statement true or false about you?

- ☐ Strongly Agree
- ☐ Agree
- ☐ Disagree
- ☐ Strongly Disagree
- ☐ Don't Know
- ☐ Refused to Answer
- ☐ No Answer

b. I doubt whether I would make a good leader. Is this statement true or false about you?

- ☐ Strongly Agree
- ☐ Agree
- ☐ Disagree
- ☐ Strongly Disagree
- ☐ Don't Know
- ☐ Refused to Answer
- ☐ No Answer

c. It is hard for me to start a conversation with strangers. Is this statement true or false about you?

- ❑ Strongly Agree
- ❑ Agree
- ❑ Disagree
- ❑ Strongly Disagree
- ❑ Don't Know
- ❑ Refused to Answer
- ❑ No Answer

Q10. Generally speaking, do you usually think of yourself as a Republican, a Democrat, an Independent, or what?

If REPUBLICAN: Would you call yourself a strong Republican or a not-so-strong Republican?

If INDEPENDENT: Do you think of yourself as closer to the Republicans or closer to the Democrats?

If DEMOCRAT: Would you call yourself a strong Democrat or a not-so-strong Democrat?

1. Strong Republican
2. Weak Republican
3. Lean Republican
4. Independent
5. Lean Democrat
6. Weak Democrat
7. Strong Democrat
8. Other (Specify): ________________________
9. Don't know
10. No answer

Q11. In politics today, do you think of yourself as a conservative, as middle of the road, as a liberal, or do you not think of yourself in these terms?

DO NOT DEFINE THESE TERMS FOR THE RESPONDENT.

1. Conservative
2. Middle of the road
3. Liberal
4. Don't think in those terms
5. Don't know
6. No answer

Q12. Would you say religion provides a little bit of guidance, some guidance, a great deal of guidance, or no guidance at all in your day-to-day living?

1. Little bit of guidance
2. Some guidance
3. Great deal of guidance
4. No guidance at all
5. Don't know (*DO NOT READ*)
6. No answer/Refused to answer (*DO NOT READ*)

Q13. How often do you attend religious services? Would you say you attend religious services more than once a week, weekly, monthly, yearly, only on special occasions, or do you never attend religious services?

1. More than once a week
2. Weekly
3. Monthly
4. Yearly
5. Only on special occasions
6. Never
7. Don't know (*DO NOT READ*)
8. No answer/Refused to answer (*DO NOT READ*)

Q14. Outside of attending religious services, how often do you pray? Would you say several times a day, once a day, several times a week, once a week, less than once a week, or never?

1. Several times a day
2. Once a day
3. Several times a week
4. Once a week
5. Less than once a week
6. Never
7. Don't know (*DO NOT READ*)
8. No answer/Refused to answer (*DO NOT READ*)

Q15. Now I would like to ask you about your religious preference. What is your religious preference? Is it protestant, Catholic, Jewish, some other religion, or no religion? (*A LIST OF WHAT MAY BE CONSIDERED PROTESTANT TO BE PROVIDED*).

1. No religion
2. Catholic
3. Jewish
4. Protestant
5. Other
6. Don't know
7. Refused to answer

IF THE PERSON HAS NO RELIGION (ATHEIST, AGNOSTIC, ETC.)—SKIP TO Q19.
IF SOME OTHER RELIGION—SKIP TO Q19.
IF JEWISH—SKIP TO Q18.
IF CATHOLIC—SKIP TO Q17.
IF PROTESTANT, ASK:

Q16. What specific denomination is that, if any? (*PROBE:* What church do you attend?)

____

IF BAPTIST: With which Baptist group is your church associated? Is it the Southern Baptist Convention, the American Baptist Churches in the U.S.A, the American Baptist Association, an independent Baptist church or some other Baptist group? IF INDEPENDENT BAPTIST: Are you affiliated with any larger Baptist group or is this strictly a local church?

IF LUTHERAN: Is this church part of the Evangelical Lutheran Church in America, the Missouri Synod, or some other Lutheran group?

IF METHODIST: Is your church part of the United Methodist Church, African Methodist Episcopal, or some other Methodist group?

IF PRESBYTERIAN: Is this the Presbyterian Church in the U.S.A. or some other Presbyterian group? [formerly United Presbyterian Church]

IF REFORMED: Is this the Christian Reformed Church, the Reformed Church in America, or some other reformed group?

IF BRETHERN: Is this the Church of the Brethren, the Plymouth Brethren, or other Brethren association?

IF CHRISTIAN: When you say "Christian," does that mean the denomination called the Christian Church Disciples of Christ or some other Christian denomination; or do you mean to say "I am just a Christian"?

IF CHURCH OF CHRIST: Is this the Church of Christ or the United Church of Christ?

IF CHURCH OF GOD: Is this the Church of God of Anderson, Indiana; the Church of God of Cleveland, Tennessee; the Church of God in Christ, or some other Church of God?

IF PENTECOSTAL, CHARISMATIC, OR HOLINESS: What kind of church is that? What is it called exactly? Is that part of a larger church or denomination?

IF EVANGELICAL: Is this Evangelical United Brethren, Evangelical Congregational, Evangelical Covenant, Evangelical Free Church, Evangelical Methodist, or just Evangelical?

Q17. Now I am going to read some statements some people might use to describe their religious opinions. For each statement, tell me whether you agree or disagree and how strongly you feel about that.

STATEMENTS

a. I enjoy reading about my religion. Do you agree or disagree? Do you feel strongly or not so strongly about that?

- ❑ Strongly Agree
- ❑ Agree
- ❑ Disagree
- ❑ Strongly Disagree
- ❑ Don't Know
- ❑ Refused to Answer
- ❑ No Answer

b. It is important to me to spend time in private thought and prayer. *READ AS NECESSARY:* Do you agree or disagree? Do you feel strongly or not so strongly about that?

- ❑ Strongly Agree
- ❑ Agree
- ❑ Disagree
- ❑ Strongly Disagree
- ❑ Don't Know
- ❑ Refused to Answer
- ❑ No Answer

c. I have often had a strong sense of God's presence. *READ AS NECESSARY:* Do you agree or disagree? Do you feel strongly or not so strongly about that?

- ❑ Strongly Agree
- ❑ Agree
- ❑ Disagree
- ❑ Strongly Disagree
- ❑ Don't Know
- ❑ Refused to Answer
- ❑ No Answer

d. I pray mainly to gain relief and protection. *READ AS NECESSARY:* Do you agree or disagree? Do you feel strongly or not so strongly about that?

- ❑ Strongly Agree
- ❑ Agree
- ❑ Disagree
- ❑ Strongly Disagree
- ❑ Don't Know
- ❑ Refused to Answer
- ❑ No Answer

e. What religion offers me most is comfort in times of trouble and sorrow. *READ AS NECESSARY:* Do you agree or disagree? Do you feel strongly or not so strongly about that?

- ❑ Strongly Agree
- ❑ Agree
- ❑ Disagree
- ❑ Strongly Disagree
- ❑ Don't Know
- ❑ Refused to Answer
- ❑ No Answer

f. I try hard to live my life according to my religious beliefs. *READ AS NECESSARY:* Do you agree or disagree? Do you feel strongly or not so strongly about that?

- ❑ Strongly Agree
- ❑ Agree
- ❑ Disagree
- ❑ Strongly Disagree
- ❑ Don't Know
- ❑ Refused to Answer
- ❑ No Answer

g. I go to church mostly to spend time with my friends. *READ AS NECESSARY:* Do you agree or disagree? Do you feel strongly or not so strongly about that?

- ❑ Strongly Agree
- ❑ Agree
- ❑ Disagree
- ❑ Strongly Disagree
- ❑ Don't Know
- ❑ Refused to Answer
- ❑ No Answer

h. I go to church mainly because I enjoy seeing people I know there. *READ AS NECESSARY:* Do you agree or disagree? Do you feel strongly or not so strongly about that?

- ❑ Strongly Agree
- ❑ Agree
- ❑ Disagree
- ❑ Strongly Disagree
- ❑ Don't Know
- ❑ Refused to Answer
- ❑ No Answer

i. My whole approach to life is based on my religion. *READ AS NECESSARY:* Do you agree or disagree? Do you feel strongly or not so strongly about that?

- ❑ Strongly Agree
- ❑ Agree
- ❑ Disagree
- ❑ Strongly Disagree
- ❑ Don't Know
- ❑ Refused to Answer
- ❑ No Answer

Q18. Which of these statements comes closest to describing your feelings about the Bible?

1. The Bible is the actual word of God and is to be taken literally, word for word.
2. The Bible is the inspired word of God, but not everything in it should be taken literally, word for word.
3. The Bible is an ancient book of fables, legends, history, and moral precepts recorded by men.
4. Don't know (*DO NOT READ*)
5. No answer/Refused to Answer (*DO NOT READ*)

Q19. *EVERYONE SHOULD ANSWER THESE QUESTIONS:* Finally, to be sure we have a representative sample of your area, we need to know a few things about you. What is the highest grade or year of school you completed?

1. Less than high school graduate
2. High school graduate/GED
3. Technical/junior college
4. Some undergraduate college credit
5. College degree/four-year degree
6. Professional or graduate school
7. Don't know (*DO NOT READ*)
8. No answer/Refused to answer (*DO NOT READ*)

Q20. In what year were you born? ______________________________

Q21. What is your race? *READ RESPONSES*

1. White
2. Black
3. Asian
4. Hispanic
5. Other (specify) ______________________________
6. Don't know (*DO NOT READ*)
7. No answer/Refused to answer (*DO NOT READ*)

Q22. Now consider all sources of income for everyone living with you in 2002, before taxes. Please stop me when I get to your income level. (*PROBE:* I just need to know the category in which your income falls.)

1. Less than $20,000
2. $20,001 to $40,000

3. $40,001 to $60,000
4. $60,001 to $80,000
5. $80,001 to $100,000
6. $100,001 to $120,000
7. More than $120,000
8. Don't know

That completes our survey. Thank you for your time and help. Goodbye.

Q23. What was the respondent's gender? (*SUPPLY BY OBSERVATION*)
1. Male
2. Female

Limitations and Assumptions

An obvious limitation was the inability to include all desired items in constructing various scales. For example, the secure personality scale uses two dogmatism items and three self-esteem items. Although this is clearly acceptable, it would of course be beneficial to include all items that have been used when measuring dogmatism and self-esteem. Ideally, because more is usually better, a seven-item scale for dogmatism and a five-to-eight item scale for self-esteem are preferable (see Sullivan et al. 1982; Marcus et al. 1995).[1] Larger scales were also preferable for the threat perception measure and the norms of democracy measures. The former measure has five adjective pairs that can be used to measure this variable, while the latter has six. In my analysis, one adjective pair is used for threat perception and two items are used to measure general norms of democracy—excluding all items regarding procedural norms of democracy. Again, although the items used have been shown to best define the construct, and it is certainly defensible, it is obviously more desirable to have a five-or-six item indicator in lieu of a two-item indicator. Because this was a phone survey, it was important to limit the length of the survey so that the average time to complete it for each respondent would not take longer than 15 minutes. Length of a phone survey is an important criterion both in terms of how much it costs to conduct and the fact that the longer it takes to administer, the less likely an individual respondent is to stay on the phone until the end.

There is also an issue of how best to define "secular." Obviously, anyone who indicates that they are atheist is easily classified as "secular." Where classification becomes an issue is for individuals who identify themselves as a Protestant or a Catholic but then have absolutely no religious commitment (e.g., no church attendance, no prayer, no religious salience). It is questionable as to whether that person should be appropriately classified as a protestant or a Catholic versus a secular classification. In my estimation, the more stringent guideline is the best. If there is no level of religious commitment, then no matter what religious preference an individual identifies with, he or she should be classified as a secular. That being said, it is very difficult to do a study that is either large enough or employs the appropriate filter questions to ensure that adequate numbers fall into each religious tradition employing this stringent of a guideline. If the study has no filter questions, then the size of the sample will need to be extremely large because many individuals identify with a religion but exhibit no religious commitment (e.g., 81 percent of Americans identify with a religion but only approximately 50 to 55 percent of Americans have any formal affiliation with a religious institution and that affiliation typically ensures at least a minimal amount of religious commitment). On the other hand, to employ filter questions—to decrease the size of the necessary sample—religion must be brought up first. In a phone survey, this is problematic generally because individual respondents will be uncomfortable with a phone survey and, therefore, less likely to agree to complete it, particularly one that deals with such controversial topics.

Because of these considerations, this research uses a less stringent definition of secular, relying solely on self-identification. Nevertheless, to account for variation in religious commitment, that variable is included in the analysis and thus controls for differences in it. Although this is not the ideal—certainly in my estimation—, it is typical. Of course, a different means of collecting the data could have been used, such as a mail survey with which more and longer surveys could have been sent out. However, a mail survey has its own set of limitations, not the least of which is a low response rate.

Appendix B

Focus Group Session Script

I. Warm up—Thanks. Discussion: Role of citizen in everyday life and influence/involvement of religion regarding it.

A. Who are you? Religious faith/denomination
B. Length of time in area and your current faith

II. Let's talk about how you act as a citizen.

A. What influences you? (*PROMPT:* Family, friends, media, clubs, faith)
B. Why that source?
C. Has it changed over time?

D. Should it be another source—primary influencer?
E. What source do you believe influences the most people in America? Why?
F. Has it changed over time?
G. Should it be another source?
H. Do you think it should be something else?

III. Zero in on faith—How does your faith affect how you act as a citizen?
A. Where did that come from—What source instilled this (family, friends, faith itself)?
B. More now than in the past? Why is that?
C. How are other people affected by their faith?
D. Where did that come from—what source instilled this (family, friends, faith itself)?
E. What are results? +/-
F. More now than in the past? Why is that?

IV. Political tolerance (*DEFINE IT FOR GROUP:* How we deal with those with whom we vehemently disagree; extending civil rights to those with whom we disagree.)
A. What is it? How strong is it in America today?
B. Is your political tolerance affected by your faith? How? Explain.
C. Does your faith affect your political decision-making? How? Explain. (Prompt with speech, petition, assembly; examples: selecting a candidate, support issues—gun control, illegal immigrants, stem-cell, maybe abortion—may be too hot a topic)
D. Would you be involved? Would you support it or support others to speak out?
E. What about other people? (*GO THROUGH SAME KINDS OF QUESTIONS*)

V. Relationship between church and state
A. How would you define it in today's society? What has influenced it?
B. Do you approve? Why or why not?
C. Has it changed over the years? How? Why?
D. What should it be? Why?

VI. Faith-based issues and programs in the United States. Tell me about any. What are they? (*PROMPT, if needed:* Stem-cell research, abortion, euthanasia)
A. Does your faith encourage your political involvement or opinions? How?
B. Are there any issues that because of your faith have caused you conflict? Explain.

VII. Talked about a lot of things—Are there changes you would like to see your faith make regarding what they say or do?

A. Do more, do less, stay the same?
B. Is your faith missing an issue that you believe is important? Should something be done or said about some issue or program?
C. How about you personally? (Based on your faith) what should be done or said about some issue or program?

VIII. What's the most important thing we have talked about tonight? What are you going away with?

Thank you and good bye!

Appendix C

"Your Help Is Needed" Flier

Your Help Is Needed

WHO are we looking for?
If you are an individual who attends services at your congregation at least once a week, you are just the person we are looking for!

WHAT do we want you to do?
Participate in a two-hour focus group with other individuals like yourself—those who attend service at ***your*** congregation at least once a week—on the topic of *Faith and Democracy.*

WHEN is the focus group session?
The focus group is on DATE at TIME p.m.

WHERE will the focus group be held?
The focus group session will be held at The Center, on the campus of Purdue University Calumet, off of 173rd Street (one block north of 80/94) between Indianapolis Boulevard and Kennedy Avenue. Parking is available directly in front of the entrance to The Center.

WHY should you participate?
In exchange for two-hours of your time, you will receive $30.00 in cash at the end of the focus group session. Refreshments are also provided.

HOW DO YOU SIGN UP?
Call Professor Marie Eisenstein at 219-614-7351 (cell phone) or 219-980-6522 (office), or E-mail her at maeisens@iun.edu.

Appendix D

Phone Script

Thank you for your willingness to participate in this study. In order for you to sign up for one of the focus group sessions, I need to get some basic contact information from you. Is that okay?

What is your first and last name?

___

What local congregation are you associated with?

___

Do you attend services at your congregation at least once a week? ______

IF NO: Thank you for contacting us; however, for our study, we need individuals who attend services at their particular congregation at least once a week.

IF YES: GO TO NEXT QUESTION

Are you 18 years of age or older? ______

IF NO: Thank you for contacting us; however, for our study, we need individuals who are a minimum of 18 years of age.

IF YES: GO TO NEXT QUESTION

In the event we need to contact you prior to the focus group session, what is the best number to reach you at?

___

Do you have an E-mail address that we may use to contact you?

___

I have you scheduled to participate in a focus group on (*DATE*) and (*TIME*). Are there any questions I can answer for you at this time?

If you have any questions that arise later or if you need to cancel your participation, please contact me at 980-6522 or by e-mail at maeisens@iun.edu. Thank you.

Appendix E

Informed Consent Statement
Study # 2004-019

INDIANA UNIVERSITY–IU NORTHWEST
INFORMED CONSENT STATEMENT
Faith and Democracy

You are invited to participate in a research study. The purpose of this study is to learn more about religious individuals, their views of American democracy, and how faith and democracy connect.

Information

Your role in this project is to participate in one two-hour focus group session. A focus group is a group of individuals with a common interest or experience that are asked to discuss and comment on questions related to a specific topic. You will be one of approximately twelve individuals in this focus group session. All the participants in this focus group session are from a local congregation, and all of them are individuals who attend their particular congregation at least once a week. The specific issue we want you to address in this focus group is can faith and political tolerance coexist?

This session will be videotaped. Your permission is required and signing this form acknowledges that you agree to be videotaped. The information from the videotape will be used for research purposes only, and your name or other identifiable information will not be used. Only the primary researcher will use information in the videotape or view the videotape. If you withdraw from the focus group before the session is finished, the information on the videotape will still be used for research purposes. At the end of the study, the videotapes will be stored for three years.

Risks

There are no foreseeable risks in participating in this study.

Benefits

Your participation in this project allows us to learn how religion and democratic government exist together.

Confidentiality

Strict confidentiality is maintained. Only the primary researcher will have access to the information. All your data will be kept in a locked file cabinet that is located in the researcher's office at Indiana University Northwest. Upon completion of the study, the videotapes will be destroyed after three years. Names will not be used in the publication of the research from this project.

Compensation

For participating in this study, you will receive $30.00 in cash at the completion of the focus group session. If you withdraw from the study prior to its completion, you will be compensated based on the rate of $15.00 an hour (in cash) prorated.

____

Subject's initials

[Page 1 of 2]

Contact

If you have questions at any time about the study or the procedures, you may contact the researcher, Dr. Marie A. Eisenstein at IU Northwest, 3400 Broadway, Gary, Ind. 46408 by phone at 219-980-6522 or by E-mail maeisens@iun.edu.

If you feel you have not been treated according to the description in this form, or your rights as a participant in research have been violated during the course of this project, you may contact Elisabeth Schultz, Human Subjects Administrator, Communications Department, IU Northwest, 3400 Broadway, Gary, Ind. 46408 by phone at 219-981-5646 or by e-mail at iunhsc@iun.edu.

Participation

Your participation in this study is voluntary; you may refuse to participate without penalty. If you decide to participate, you may withdraw from the study at any time without penalty and without loss of benefits to which you are otherwise entitled. If you withdraw from the study before the focus group session is finished, the data collected will still be videotaped and used for research purposes.

Consent

I have read this form and received a copy of it. I have had all my questions answered to my satisfaction. I understand and agree to be videotaped during the focus group session. I understand and agree that if I withdraw from the session that videotaping will not be stopped or erased.

Subject's signature ______________________________

Date ________________

Consent form date: 11/09/05

Appendix F

Political Attitudes Questionnaire

This questionnaire contains several questions concerning your political attitudes within American politics. This is an anonymous survey, so do not write your name on it. We would appreciate your honest and thoughtful answers on the questions contained here. No one will ever be able to identify your particular answers, so please be as honest as you can. Please answer all questions in the order they are presented.
If you have any questions, please ask the survey administrator. Thank you for your participation. We appreciate your help with this project.

Instructions: Please clearly indicate your answer by circling the response that best answers the question for you.

First, we would like to ask about your attitude toward the government.

Section A

1. Overall, do you approve or disapprove of the way the United States Congress is handling its job?

1	2	3	4	5
Strongly Approve	Approve	Neutral	Disapprove	Strongly Disapprove

2. Overall, do you approve or disapprove of the way the President is handling his job?

1	2	3	4	5
Strongly Approve	Approve	Neutral	Disapprove	Strongly Disapprove

3. How do you think today's Congress is performing compared to the Congresses of the past?

1	2	3	4
Poor	Only Fair	Good	Excellent

4. Overall, how would you rate the ability of Congress to work with the President of the United States in passing laws?

1	2	3	4
Poor	Only Fair	Good	Excellent

5. Overall, how would you rate the job the federal government, as a whole, is doing?

1	2	3	4
Poor	Only Fair	Good	Excellent

6. On a ten-point thermometer scale, how do you feel about political parties? The higher the number, the warmer or more favorable you feel toward political parties. The lower the number, the colder or less favorable you feel toward political parties. You would answer 5 if you feel neither warm nor cold toward political parties.

1	2	3	4	5	6	7	8	9	10
Cold				Neutral					Warm

Please tell us whether you agree or disagree with the following statements.
(Note to readers: All variations of Questions 7, 8, and 9 are shown here, but each survey had only one variation of these questions depending on which context group each student was randomly assigned into.)

7. Homosexual marriage should not be allowed because it disrupts society. (social context)
Homosexual marriage should not be allowed. (neutral context)
Homosexual marriage should not be allowed because it goes against God. (moral context)

1	2	3	4	5
Strongly Agree	Somewhat Agree	Neither Agree nor Disagree	Somewhat Disagree	Strongly Disagree

8. Stem-cell research should not be allowed because it is dangerous to society. (social context)
Stem-cell research should not be allowed. (neutral context)
Stem-cell research should not be allowed because it is morally wrong. (moral context)

1	2	3	4	5
Strongly Agree	Somewhat Agree	Neither Agree nor Disagree	Somewhat Disagree	Strongly Disagree

9. Abortion should not be allowed because it is damaging to our society. (social context)
Abortion should not be allowed. (neutral context)
Abortion should not be allowed because it destroys life. (moral context)

1	2	3	4	5
Strongly Agree	Somewhat Agree	Neither Agree nor Disagree	Somewhat Disagree	Strongly Disagree

In the next set of questions, we would like you to tell us your attitudes toward certain groups.

10. In the United States today, do you think that terrorists are a big threat, a moderate threat, or no threat at all to Americans?

A Big Threat   A Moderate Threat   No Threat At All

11. Listed below are some different groups you may have heard of. Please indicate which group you like the least from this list:
Socialists
Ku Klux Klan members
Pro-choice people
Pro-life people

12. Below is a list of four more groups. Please indicate which group you like the least from this list.
Atheists
Homosexuals
Religious fundamentalists
Feminists

13. Taking the two groups you just indicated you like the least from Questions 11 and 12, please indicate which of those two groups is your least-liked group. Please write your answer in the space provided.

____

Using your answer to Question 13, please answer the following list of statements. For each statement, circle the response that best answers the question for you.

14. Your Answer to Question 13 should be banned from running for public office in the U.S.

1	2	3	4	5
Strongly Agree	Somewhat Agree	Neither Agree nor Disagree	Somewhat Disagree	Strongly Disagree

15. Your Answer to Question 13 should be allowed to teach in public schools.

1	2	3	4	5
Strongly Agree	Somewhat Agree	Neither Agree nor Disagree	Somewhat Disagree	Strongly Disagree

16. Your Answer to Question 13 should be outlawed.

1	2	3	4	5
Strongly Agree	Somewhat Agree	Neither Agree nor Disagree	Somewhat Disagree	Strongly Disagree

17. Your Answer to Question 13 should be allowed to hold public rallies.

1	2	3	4	5
Strongly Agree	Somewhat Agree	Neither Agree nor Disagree	Somewhat Disagree	Strongly Disagree

In the next set of questions, we would like you to answer some basic descriptive information about yourself.

Section B

1. Generally, speaking, do you usually think of yourself as a Republican, a Democrat, or an Independent?

1	2	3	4	5	6	7
Strong Democrat	Democrat	Weak Democrat	Independent	Weak Republican	Republican	Strong Republican

2. What is your year of birth? ____________________________

3. What is your race? White Black Asian Hispanic
Other: ______________________

4. What is your gender? Female Male

5. Lots of things come up that keep people from attending religious services even if they want to. Thinking about your life these days, apart from occasional weddings, baptisms, or funerals, how often do you attend religious services?

1	2	3	4	5	6
More Than Once a Week	Weekly	Monthly	Yearly	Only on Special Occasions	Never

6. What is your religious affiliation?
Protestant
Catholic
Jewish
None
Other: ______________________

If your answer is Protestant, please answer Question 6a. Otherwise, skip to Question 7.

6a. What specific denomination or church is that? Please write your answer in the space provided. If you are unsure, leave blank and go to Question 7.

____

7. What is your family's annual income?
$0 to $20,000
$21 to $40,000
$41 to $60,000
$61 to $80,000
$81 to$100,000
$101,000 to $120,000
$121,000 +

8. What point on this scale best describes your political views?

1	2	3	4	5	6	7
Extremely Liberal	Liberal	Weak Liberal	Moderate	Weak Conservative	Conservative	Extremely Conservative

THANK YOU VERY MUCH FOR YOUR PARTICIPATION!!

Notes

INTRODUCTION

1 According to Schotten and Stevens (1996), what they call the separationist test, embodied in the Everson decision in 1947, was replaced in 1971 by the *Lemon* test. The *Lemon* test was a three-pronged test for determining whether the establishment clause had been violated. The *Lemon* test came under attack because it yielded inconsistent and varying results partly because it could take on either an accommodationist or a separationist interpretation.

2 Keep in mind, even within each of these venues, the topic can be further subdivided and researched from, for example, a Marxist perspective, a capitalist perspective, a feminist perspective, a secular perspective, and so on.

3 In fact, as I argue in chapter 1, even within mainstream political science and the subfield of religion and politics within political science, two divergent literature bases dealing with religion, liberal democracy, and political tolerance have developed quite separately and distinctly from one another. Thus, this fracturing of academic venues occurs within academic disciplines as well as between academic disciplines.

CHAPTER 1

1 I should note that the discussion about whether political tolerance is always acceptable is completely separate and unique than any discussion regarding social tolerance. Social tolerance

may be understood, briefly and easily, as the "simple etiquette of public life and is crucial to citizens' quality of life, especially in a pluralistic democracy" (Stetson & Conti 2005, 170). In contrast, political tolerance, involves the de jure or legal protections of civil liberties. Political tolerance is usually enforced by the state; social tolerance is usually enforced through social norms, such as peer pressure.

2 Hence, Madison's famous quote from Federalist 51: "If men were angels, no government would be necessary. If angels were to govern men, neither external nor internal controls on government would be necessary."

3 For a more detailed and thorough discussion of the limits of political tolerance and the three different theories of democratic governance that influence the limits of political tolerance, see pp. 7–25 in Sullivan, Piereson, and Marcus (1982).

4 Portions of this section first appeared in *Political Behavior* 28 (2006): 327–48.

5 Throughout this discussion, I often make use of the terms "democracy" and "liberal democracy." When referring to democracy in the modern-day United States, I am specifically referring to liberal democracy. Democracy by itself, representative or direct, is strictly a political decision-making process by citizens (e.g., Greek democratic city-states). In the discussion of strict political decision-making, there is no concern or need for tolerance. On the other hand, liberal democracy is not just a decision-making process; it is also a theory of how to attain truth. Analogous to the market economy, liberal democracy argues that the "marketplace of ideas" will give rise over time to the best possible decision-making in a political system. Therefore, all ideas must be allowed to enter the marketplace to compete for an individual's loyalty; it then becomes necessary for government to protect the conditions that make this idea "marketplace" possible. Those conditions are exemplified by the U.S. Constitution and its first ten amendments (the Bill of Rights). The underlying assumption of these rights is the attitude or practice of toleration. Therefore, in the contemporary discussion of American democracy, one generally assumes this to be liberal democracy.

6 Religious tradition is different from mere denominational affiliation. Denomination refers to a specific affiliation such as Catholic,

Baptist, Lutheran, Episcopalian, and Methodist. Religious tradition refers to "a group of denominations and movements that share common practices, beliefs, and origins" (Layman & Green 1998, 2).

7 It should be noted that Nunn, Crockett, and Williams in *Tolerance for Nonconformity* conducted their research in an identical fashion to Stouffer's. This was very important because Stouffer's work represented the first comprehensive and methodologically advanced work for his day on American tolerance. Thus, any attempt to chart change over the previous two decades must of necessity begin with that work.

8 Sullivan, Piereson, and Marcus (1982) made a convincing argument about the requirement to disentangle assessments of tolerance toward groups versus tolerance of actions taken by those groups. Asking a respondent about his or her willingness to tolerate teaching or speaking by a communist taps not only attitudes toward the action (speaking) but also attitudes toward communists as a group. Sullivan and the other authors also convincingly argued that the original items used by Stouffer ([1955] 1992) and subsequently adopted by the General Social Surveys (GSS) to measure tolerance were ideologically biased toward individuals who did not have strong (moral) objections toward atheists, communists, or socialists. Because the items asked about willingness to extend civil liberties toward communists, atheists, and socialists, the critique is that individuals who are sympathetic to those groups will of course be more willing to extend civil liberties to them, but this does not make those individuals more tolerant than others. To correct for these problems, Sullivan and the others developed a content-controlled measure (alternatively called a "least-liked" measure). Their work brought into question the results from research projects that used a political tolerance measure that was plagued by content bias.

9 Using their content-controlled measure, Sullivan, Piereson, and Marcus were the first scholars to suggest that little difference existed between the tolerance levels of protestants, Catholics, and Jews. These results represented a radical departure from previous research, which had consistently indicated that Jews were more tolerant than protestants and Catholics.

10 Beatty and Walter (1984), as well as Wilcox and Jelen (1990), modified their political tolerance measure to best accommodate the

critique of Sullivan, Piereson, and Marcus. The authors assessed the tolerance for each respondent for each of the target groups (communists, atheists, etc.). Then, they constructed a general tolerance index that represented each respondent's lowest tolerance score, thereby approximating the respondent's "least-liked" group.

11 Wilcox and Jelen (1990) did control for perceived communist threat. However, this is not a general measure of threat perception, and they were not able to control for perceived communist threat throughout their study.

12 Sullivan, Piereson, and Marcus (1982) were the first scholars to successfully argue for a measure of psychological insecurity (termed "secure personality" in this text). This psychological variable was then included in other scholarly studies, including but not limited to, Davis (1995); Marcus et al. (1995); and Peffley et al. (2001).

CHAPTER 2

1 Portions of this chapter first appeared in *Political Behavior* 28 (2006): 327–48.

2 Religion is conceptualized as having three distinct, yet interrelated dimensions: religious belief, religious belonging, and religious behavior (Wuthnow 1988; Jelen 1991; Carwardine 1993; Kellstedt 1993; Kellstedt et al. 1996; Layman & Green 1998).

3 Structural equation modeling allows for a series of regression equations to be not just pictorially modeled but also tested "statistically in a simultaneous analysis of the entire system of variables to determine the extent to which it is consistent with the data" (Byrne 2001, 3).

4 The survey had a 58 percent maximum response rate calculated using AAPOR (American Association for Public Opinion Research) Response Rate 6 (RR6). The AAPOR has many different ways in which response rates can be calculated. The maximum response rate (RR6), a modified version of RR3, minimizes the denominator by not including cases of "unknown" eligibility (such as no answers and busy signals). The various definitions used by AAPOR in calculating response rates can be viewed at http://www.aapor.org (search for "Standard Definitions").

5 Visually, figure 2.1, which is a structural equation model, looks as though it might also be called a "path analysis." In broad terms, the difference is one of variable measurement. Path analyses use

single indicator variables; in contrast, structural equation modeling allows for latent variables that are measured by multiple observed indicators.

6 There is a debate about what is meant by the salience of religion (Guth & Green 1993). The empirical evidence supports the inclusion of this item as a measure of religious commitment/behavior. For example, in a principal components analysis of these three items, the religious salience item loads on the same factor as the church attendance and frequency of prayer items (Eisenstein 2006, 18). Layman (1997, 291), using the same three items to measure religious commitment/behavior, demonstrated that these indicators load on a single factor and, in an analysis of several National Election Studies (NES) data sets, obtained alpha reliability coefficients ranging from .70 to .75. For the same three items, Kellstedt (1993) obtained an alpha reliability coefficient of .74; Layman and Green (1998) obtained an alpha reliability coefficient of .81.

7 Party identification had seven potential response categories into which a respondent could be classified (Question 10 in appendix A). These categories were: strong Republican, weak Republican, lean Republican, independent, lean Democrat, weak Democrat, and strong Democrat. For my purposes here, I consolidated this into three categories: Republican, Democrat, and Independent. Strong Republican, weak Republican, and lean Republican were consolidated into one category. The same was done for strong Democrat, weak Democrat, and lean Democrat.

8 In Lake County (May 2003), the following cities had mayoral elections: Crown Point, East Chicago, Gary, Hammond, Hobart, Lake Station, and Whiting. This information is taken from the Indiana Secretary of State (Election Division) Web site (http://www.in.gov/sos/elections/elections/index.html).

9 In this dataset, 57 respondents can be classified as black protestant. Of the remaining 34 black respondents in the data set, 8 are classified as Catholic, 13 are classified as evangelical protestant, and 7 are classified as mainline protestant. Of the 60 Hispanic respondents, 45 are classified as Catholics, 9 as evangelical protestant, and none as mainline protestant.

10 Sullivan et al. (1982) tested for a direct relationship between political conservatism and political tolerance. Their results were a weak path coefficient that was not statistically significant,

and they deleted this path from the remainder of their analyses. For comparative purposes, the model here was estimated with a direct path from political conservatism to political tolerance and the results were similar; a weak path coefficient (-.01) that is not statistically significant.

11 I tested the models with a direct path between education and political tolerance to find out whether this changed the relationship between religious commitment and political tolerance. It did not; neither was the path co-efficient of any consequence substantially or statistically.

CHAPTER 3

1 Although Bolce and De Maio use the term "fundamentalist," I use the term "Christian conservative." I do so because of the way in which Bolce and De Maio coded a fundamentalist versus a nonfundamentalist. For these authors, anyone belonging to an evangelical denomination and who indicated a belief that the Bible is the infallible word of God was classified as fundamentalist. Because in contemporary America, fundamentalist has come to be associated with violent fringe groups (and just as often associated with Islamic fringe groups), I use the less-negative "Christian conservative." Furthermore, fundamentalism, at least within academic research, is generally defined as a fringe group. (Evangelicalism, with its belief in the infallibility of the Bible, is not technically considered a fringe group in American society.) Twenty-five percent of all Americans who express a belief in God identify as evangelicals, and a large percentage of those believe that the Bible is the infallible word of God (which is distinct from asking whether the Bible should be taken literally).

2 I would like to thank the Center for Regional Excellence in the area of "Cultural Discovery and Learning" associated with Indiana University Northwest for the funding needed to conduct the focus group research necessary for this chapter.

3 The Center for Regional Excellence in the area of "Cultural Discovery and Learning" associated with Indiana University Northwest funded the cost of these focus groups. In agreeing to do so, the research had to have a local connection; in this instance, congregants from surrounding communities were used.

4 Three of the religious traditions discussed in this chapter are consistent with the traditions I analyzed in chapter 2. These were evangelical protestant, mainline protestant, and Catholic.

However, in chapter 2, I was not able to include an analysis of the black protestant tradition, but I include that tradition in this chapter.

5 Within traditional religion and politics literature, religion is conceptualized as having three distinct, yet interrelated dimensions: religious belief, religious belonging, and religious behavior (Jelen 1991; Kellstedt 1993; Kellstedt et al. 1996; Layman & Green 1998). Religious tradition is a means of measuring the concept of religious belonging. Thus, in determining the makeup of my focus group participants, I used religious tradition as a means of determining who would be included in each of the four focus groups. Technically, there were four separate churches that participated. Each of the churches was of a different denomination and each denomination corresponded to a particular religious tradition. Religious tradition refers to "a group of denominations and movements that share common practices, beliefs and origins" (Layman & Green 1998, 2). Although "denomination" denotes a particular affiliation with a single religious institution, religious tradition is the aggregation of numerous single religious institutions into a single category. I incorporate the term "religious tradition" here to be consistent with previous chapters.

6 The professional focus group firm contracted to conduct the actual focus groups was Survey Research Services, located in Urbana-Champaign, Illinois.

7 The priest at the Catholic parish informed me that he had the project mentioned along with other church news during at least one of the church's scheduled services.

8 Transcripts of the focus group sessions are available from the author.

CHAPTER 4

1 This situation is what some scholars have termed the "culture war." For a review of this, please see Hunter 1991 and 1994. This study does not focus on the culture war per se, but the issues associated with the "culture war" are also some of the same religion and public opinion issues relevant to this review.

2 Please see chapter 1 for a discussion of the concept of political tolerance in greater detail.

3 Fulton, Gorsuch, and Maynard (1999) did not study political tolerance. Rather, it was a study of antipathy (or prejudice) in rela-

tion to religious fundamentalism. My point in using this study as a reference is that it argues for a moral versus a social assessment of attitudes toward homosexuality. Given the religiously based attitudes that many individuals have about issues such as abortion, stem-cell research, and homosexual marriage, such a distinction is entirely appropriate and, therefore, incorporated into the study.

4 This survey-based experiment is similar to a split-ballot survey experiment, with two exceptions: (1) I used three variations of the survey (not two); and (2) split-ballot survey experiments are typically done with a random telephone survey (e.g., Sullivan et al. 1978; Schuman & Bobo 1988). I was able to randomly assign students into one of the three survey categories (social, neutral, and moral), but my initial design was not a random sample telephone survey.

5 The regional campus on which the survey was conducted is located in Lake County, Indiana. Furthermore, this regional campus is a nonresidential campus—meaning its students are drawn from the local population. There was, however, a gender disparity in my sample. In Lake County, Indiana, 51.8 percent of the population is female and 48.2 percent of the population is male. In my sample, 67.9 percent of the respondents were female while 30.8 percent of the respondents were male. This breakdown mirrors the composition of this particular regional campus on which 70 percent of all students are female. All Lake County, Indiana, statistics are drawn from U.S. census data.

6 A one-way ANOVA allows me to test for the statistical significance of the differences of the mean scores of two or more groups. In this instance, there are three groups (social, neutral, and moral).

7 When conducting an analysis of variance, eta-squared is to ANOVA what R-squared is to regression analysis. It provides the explanatory power of the model (e.g., explained variance).

8 Consistent with the qualitative data from chapter 3; remember, I was not able to include the black protestant tradition in the empirical analyses of chapter 2.

9 As indicated previously in this chapter, religious tradition and religious commitment (e.g., the belonging and behavior dimensions of religion, respectively) influence issue attitude opinions. In addition, as discussed in chapters 1 and 2, religious tradition

and religious commitment are two of the three dimensions of religion (e.g., belief, belonging, and behavior) important in the study of religion and politics. Therefore, examining differentiation based upon religious tradition as well as religious commitment is pertinent.

10 As an aside, one may think that I should have looked solely at the influence of religious tradition or religious commitment on issue attitude. However, that is not appropriate with the data for this chapter because not all respondents were asked the same issue-attitude questions, because the data is from a survey-based experiment in which the issue-attitude questions were systematically manipulated (creating three different categories that must be used throughout this analysis).

11 The twelve different levels or categories for this variable are: social-Catholic, social-black protestant, social-mainline, social-evangelical, neutral-Catholic, neutral-black protestant, neutral-mainline, neutral-evangelical, moral-Catholic, moral-black protestant, moral-mainline, and moral-evangelical.

12 In this analysis, I cannot include the covariate religious commitment. The reason for this is because post-hoc tests, which indicate the means that are significantly different (e.g., is the social context mean score significantly different than the moral context mean score, for example), cannot be computed with a covariate predictor in the model. Put differently, post-hoc tests are for fixed between-subject factors only. Thus, the religious commitment variable had to be excluded. The end result is that I could only conduct a one-way ANOVA to determine which groups had significantly different means. In a factorial ANOVA without religious commitment as a covariate, the homosexual marriage issue attitude was the only model in which an interaction between context and religious tradition was statistically significant (consistent with the results reported here).

13 Briefly, this approach requires that respondents be allowed to identify their "most disliked" group from among a list of "extremist" groups that represent the right as well as the left, in addition to groups that do not necessarily fall on the left-right continuum.

14 In chapter 2, the survey used had five political tolerance questions. The one used for this chapter had four political tolerance questions. The decision to use four political tolerance questions

is purely pragmatic. I wanted to construct a survey that could reasonably be completed in ten minutes or less by respondents to make it more likely that respondents would complete the entire survey. The question not asked here (but was asked in the other date set) is: [Least-Liked Group] should be allowed to make a public speech. Of all five political tolerance questions in chapter 2, the question not included here had the lowest factor loading in a principal components analysis. Furthermore, Cronbach's alpha reliability coefficient for the four political tolerance items used in this chapter is .743 (the reliability coefficient for the five items used in chapter 2 is .78), showing that these four items are a reliable measure of the underlying concept, political tolerance.

15 Before conducting this factorial ANOVA, I ran a one-way ANOVA to examine whether there was a difference between the means of political tolerance based on the social, neutral, and moral contexts. There was not. The F statistic for the one-way ANOVA analysis was .525 (significance of .592) and context provided no ability to explain level of political tolerance (eta-squared was .000). I also tested the same factorial ANOVA presented in table 4.6 while including religious commitment as a covariate. Doing so did not alter the results; furthermore, religious commitment did not achieve statistical significance in any model tested.

16 I also tested this factorial ANOVA and included religious commitment as a covariate; doing so did not substantively or statistically alter the results presented in table 4.7.

CHAPTER 5

1 Hedges begins his book by saying that he is talking about only those fundamentalists who subscribe to R. J. Rushdoony and his book called "The Institutes of Biblical Law." However, the examples and portraits of Christians throughout his book are not accurate reflections of Christians who subscribe to Rushdoony or his book. Rather, they are a portrait of contemporary evangelical Christians who are not the intolerant militants (as supported by my work here) that Hedges would lead one to believe. Rather, they are evangelicals who listen to Christian rock music and buy Starbuck's coffee. To use a nonscientific standard, in the hundreds of evangelical services I have personally attended at churches from one end of the United States to the other, I have never once heard Rushdoony or his book mentioned.

2 The following Pew Research Center Publications Web pages provide more information about these findings: For "Frequent Church-Goers Are Happier" go to http://pewresearch.org/pubs/?ChartID=12 and for "How Income and Church Attendance Affects Happiness" go to http://pewresearch.org/pubs/?ChartsID=5. A copy of the entire report (as well as numerous other reports) can be downloaded from http://pewresearch.org/pubs/?PubID=301. In the event that this page ever goes offline or is no longer available, a copy of the report can be obtained from the author.

APPENDIX A

1 I should note, however, that the three items scale used to measure self-esteem in this research is based on the work of Peffley et al. (2001), which uses the California Personality Inventory (CPI). For comparison purposes, the ability to incorporate the entire set of items used by Sullivan et al. (1982) and Marcus et al. (1995) would have been beneficial.

References

Adorno, T. W., Else Frenkel-Brunswick, Daniel J. Levinson, and R. Nevitt Sanford. 1950. *The Authoritarian Personality.* New York: Harper & Brothers.

Alley, Robert S. 1999. *The Constitution and Religion: Leading Supreme Court Cases on Church and State.* New York: Prometheus Books.

Allport, Gordon W. 1954. *The Nature of Prejudice.* Menlo Park, Calif.: Addison-Wesley.

Armstrong, Karen. 1996. *Jerusalem: One City, Three Faiths.* New York: Alfred A. Knopf.

Beatty, Kathleen Murphy and Oliver Walter. 1984. "Religious Preference and Practice: Reevaluating Their Impact on Political Tolerance." *The Public Opinion Quarterly* 48: 318–29.

Bolce, Louis and Gerald De Maio. 1999a. "Religious Outlook, Culture War Politics, and Antipathy toward Christian Fundamentalists." *The Public Opinion Quarterly* 63(1): 29–61.

Bolce, Louis and Gerald De Maio. 1999b. "The Anti-Christian Fundamentalist Factor in Contemporary Politics." *The Public Opinion Quarterly* 63(4): 508–42.

Briand, Michael K. 1993. "Where Do You Get Your Ideas? A Reply to Nelson Polsby." PS: Political Science and Politics, 26(3):540–43.

Butler, Jon, Grant Wacker, and Randall Balmer. 2003. *Religion in American Life.* New York: Oxford University Press.

Byrne, Barbara M. 2001. *Structural Equation Modeling with AMOS: Basic Concepts, Applications, and Programming.* Mahwah, N.J.: Lawrence Erlbaum Associates.

Capps, Walter H., ed. 1972. *Ways of Understanding Religion*. New York: Macmillan.

Carwardine, Richard. 1993. *Evangelicals and Politics in Antebellum America*. New Haven: Yale University Press.

Conover, Pamela and Virginia Gray. 1981. "Political Activists and Conflict over Abortion and ERA: Pro-Family versus Pro-Woman." Presented at the 1981 annual meeting of the Midwest Political Science Association, Chicago.

Conover, Pamela Johnston, Ivor M. Crewe, and Donald D. Searing. 1991. "The Nature of Citizenship in the United States and Great Britain: Empirical Comments on Theoretical Themes." *The Journal of Politics* 53(3): 800–32.

Converse, Phillip E. 1974. "Some Priority Variables in Comparative Electoral Research." In *Electoral Behavior.* Edited by Richard Rose. New York: Free Press, 727–45.

Corbett, Michael. 1982. *Political Tolerance in America: Freedom and Equality in Public Attitudes*. New York: Longman.

Crick, Bernard. 1973. *Political Theory and Practice*. New York: Basic Books.

Cutler, Stephen J. and Robert L. Kaufman. 1975. "Cohort Changes in Political Attitudes: Tolerance of Ideological Conformity." *Public Opinion Quarterly* 39: 69–81.

Davis, Darren W. 1995. "Exploring Black Political Intolerance." *Political Behavior* 17(1): 1–22.

Davis, James A. 1975. "Communism, Conformity, Cohorts, and Categories: American Tolerance in 1954 and 1972–73." *American Journal of Sociology* 81: 491–513.

Davis, Darren W. and B. D. Silver. 2004. "Civil Liberties vs. Security: Public Opinion in the Context of the Terrorist Attacks on America." *American Journal of Political Science* 48(1): 28–46.

de Gruchy, John W. 2004. "Democracy." In *The Blackwell Companion to Political Theology*. Edited by Peter Scott and William T. Cavanaugh. Blackwell Publishing, 439–54.

Dreisbach, Daniel L. 2002. *Thomas Jefferson and the Wall of Separation between Church and State*. New York and London: New York University Press.

Eisenstein, Marie A. 2005. "Religion, Values, and Freedom of Speech in Public Places." *Public Administration Times* 28(8): 5.

Eisenstein, Marie A. 2006. "Religious Motivation vs. Traditional Religiousness: Bridging the Gap between Religion and Politics and the Psychology of Religion." *Interdisciplinary Journal of Research on Religion* 2: article 2: http://www.religjournal.com.

Erskine, Hazel and Richard L. Siegel. 1975. "Civil Liberties and the American Public." *Journal of Social Issues* 31(2): 13–29.

Filsinger, Erik. 1976. "Tolerance of Non-Believers: A Cross-Tabular and Log Linear Analysis of Some Religious Correlates." *Review of Religious Research* 17: 232–40.

Fulton, Aubyn S., Richard L. Gorsuch, and Elizabeth A. Maynard. 1999. "Religious Orientation, Antihomosexual Sentiment, and Fundamentalism among Christians." *Journal for the Scientific Study of Religion* 38(1): 14–22.

Gibson, James L. and Richard D. Bingham. 1985. *Civil Liberties and Nazis: The Skokie Free-Speech Controversy.* New York: Praeger.

Gibson, James L. 1986. "Pluralistic Intolerance in America." *American Politics Quarterly* 14: 267–93.

Gibson, James L. 1989. "The Structure of Attitudinal Tolerance in the United States." *British Journal of Political Science* 19: 562–70.

Gibson, James L. 1992. "Alternative Measures of Political Tolerance: Must Tolerance Be 'Least-Liked'?" *American Journal of Political Science* 36(2): 560–77.

Gibson, James L. 2006. "Enigmas of Intolerance: Fifty Years after Stouffer's Communism, Conformity, and Civil Liberties." *Perspectives on Politics* 4(1): 21–34.

Gibson, James L. and Amanda Gouws. 2000. "Social Identities and Political Intolerance: Linkages within the South African Mass Public." *American Journal of Political Science* 44(2): 278–92.

Greeley, Andrew M. 1991. *The Catholic Myth: The Behavior and Belief of American Catholics.* New York: Scribner's.

Green, John C., James L. Guth, Lyman A. Kellstedt, and Corwin E. Smidt. 1994. "Uncivil Challenges? Support for Civil Liberties among Religious Activists." *The Journal of Political Science* 22: 25–49.

Guth, James L. and John C. Green. 1993. "Salience: The Core Concept?" In *Rediscovering the Religious Factor in American Politics.* Edited by David C. Leege and Lyman A. Kellstedt. Armonk, N.Y.: M. E. Sharpe, 157–74.

Guth, James L., Corwin E. Smidt, Lyman A. Kellstedt, and John C. Green. 1993. "The Sources of Antiabortion Attitudes." *American Politics Quarterly* 21: 65–80.

Hedges, Chris. 2006. *American Fascists: The Christian Right and the War on America.* New York: Free Press.

Hibbing, John R. and Elizabeth Theiss-Morse. 1995. *Congress as Public Enemy: Public Attitudes toward American Political Institutions.* Cambridge: Cambridge University Press.

Hunter, James Davison. 1991. *Culture Wars: The Struggle to Define America.* New York: Basic Books.

Hunter, James Davison. 1994. *Before the Shooting Begins: Searching for Democracy in America's Culture War.* New York: Free Press.

Jelen, Ted G. 1991. *The Political Mobilization of Religious Beliefs.* Westport, Conn.: Praeger.

Jerolmack, Colin and Douglas Porpora. 2004. "Religion, Rationality, and Experience: A Response to the New Rational Choice Theory of Religion." *Sociological Theory* 22(1): 140–60.

Kellstedt, Lyman A. 1993. "Religion, the Neglected Variable: An Agenda for Future Research on Religion and Political Behavior." In *Rediscovering the Religious Factor in American Politics.* Edited by David C. Leege and Lyman A. Kellstedt. Armonk, N.Y.: M. E. Sharpe, 273–303.

Kellstedt, Lyman A. and John C. Green. 1993. "Knowing God's Many People: Denominational Preference and Political Behavior." In *Rediscovering the Religious Factor in American Politics.* Edited by David C. Leege and Lyman A. Kellstedt. Armonk, N.Y.: M. E. Sharpe, 53–71.

Kellstedt, Lyman A., John C. Green, James L. Guth, and Corwin E. Smidt. 1996. "Grasping the Essentials: The Social Embodiment of Religion and Political Behavior." In *Religion and the Culture Wars.* Edited by John C. Green, James L. Guth, Corwin E. Smidt, and Lyman A. Kellstedt. Lanham, Md.: Rowman & Littlefield, 174–92.

Kinder, Donald R. and Thomas R. Palfrey. 1993. "On Behalf of an Experimental Political Science." In *Experimental Foundations of Political Science.* Edited by Donald R. Kinder and Thomas R. Palfrey. Ann Arbor: University of Michigan Press, 1–39.

King Jr., Martin Luther. 1964. "Letter from Birmingham Jail." In *Why We Can't Wait.* New York: Mentor Books.

Kirk, Russell. 2002. *The American Cause.* Wilmington, Del.: ISI Books, [1957].

Kraynak, Robert P. 2001. *Christian Faith and Modern Democracy: God and Politics in the Fallen World.* Notre Dame, Ind.: University of Notre Dame Press.

Krueger, Richard A. and Mary Anne Casey. 2000. *Focus Groups: A Practical Guide for Applied Research.* 3rd ed. Thousand Oaks, Calif.: Sage.

Layman, Geoffrey C. 1997. "Religion and Political Behavior in the United States: The Impact of Beliefs, Affiliation, and Commitment from 1980 to 1994." *Public Opinion Quarterly* 61: 288–316.

Layman, Geoffrey C. and John C. Green. 1998. "The Changing Religious Voter: The Political Impact of Belonging, Believing, and Behaving." Delivered at the 1998 Annual Meeting of the Midwest Political Science Association (April 23–25): Chicago, Ill.

Leege, David C. and Lyman A. Kellstedt. 1993. "Religious Worldviews and Political Philosophies: Capturing Theory in a Grand Manner through Empirical Data." In *Rediscovering the Religious Factor in American Politics*. Edited by David C. Leege and Lyman A. Kellstedt. Armonk, N.Y.: M. E. Sharpe, 216–31.

Leege, David C., Kenneth D. Wald, and Lyman A. Kellstedt. 1993. "The Public Dimension of Private Devotionalism." In *Rediscovering the Religious Factor in American Politics*. Edited by David C. Leege and Lyman A. Kellstedt. Armonk, N.Y.: M. E. Sharpe, 139–56.

Lippman, Walter. 1995. *Essays in the Public Philosophy*. Boston: Little, Brown.

Marcus, George E., John L. Sullivan, Elizabeth Theiss-Morse, and Sandra L. Wood. 1995. *With Malice toward Some: How People Make Civil Liberties Judgments*. Cambridge: Cambridge University Press.

Marsden, George M. 1980. *Fundamentalism and American Culture: The Shaping of Twentieth-Century Evangelism, 1870–1925*. New York: Oxford University Press.

Marsden, George M. 1997. *The Outrageous Idea of Christian Scholarship*. New York: Oxford University Press.

McClosky, Herbert. 1964. "Consensus and Ideology in American Politics." *American Political Science Review* 58: 361–82.

McClosky, Herbert and Alida Brill. 1983. *Dimensions of Tolerance*. New York: Sage.

Merton, Robert K., Marjorie Fiske, and Patricia L. Kendall. 1956. *The Focused Interview*. Glencoe, Ill.: Free Press.

Morgan, David L. 1988. *Focus Groups as Qualitative Research*. Newbury Park, Calif.: Sage.

Mueller, John. 1988. "Trends in Political Tolerance." *Public Opinion Quarterly* 52: 1–25.

Murphy, Andrew. 1997. "Tolerance, Toleration, and the Liberal Tradition." *Polity* 29(4): 593–623.

Nunn, Clyde Z., Harry J. Crockett Jr., and J. Allen Williams Jr. 1978. *Tolerance for Nonconformity*. San Francisco: Jossey-Bass.

Olsen, Laura R. and Ted G. Jelen. 1998. *The Religious Dimension of Political Behavior: A Critical Analysis and Annotated Bibliography.* Westport, Conn.: Greenwood Press.

O'Neil, Robert M. 1999. "The 'Wall of Separation' and Thomas Jefferson's View on Religious Liberty." *The William and Mary Quarterly* 56(4): 791–94.

Peffley, Mark, Pia Knigge, and Jon Hurwitz. 2001. "A Multiple Values Model of Political Tolerance." *Political Research Quarterly* 54(2): 379–406.

Polsby, Nelson. 1993. "Where Do You Get Your Ideas?" *PS: Political Science and Politics* 26(3): 83–87.

Protho, James W. and Charles W. Grigg. 1960. "Fundamental Principles of Democracy: Bases of Agreement and Disagreement." *Journal of Politics* 22: 276–94.

Reid Jr., Charles J. 2003. "The Religious Conscience and the State in U.S. Constitutional Law, 1789–2001." In *Religion Returns to the Public Square: Faith and Policy in America.* Edited by Hugh Heclo and Wilfred M. McClay. Washington, D.C. and Baltimore, Md.: Woodrow Wilson Center Press and the John Hopkins University Press, 63–110.

Rokeach, Milton. 1960. *The Open and Closed Mind.* New York: Basic Books.

Schotten, Peter and Dennis Stevens. 1996. *Religion, Politics, and the Law: Commentaries and Controversies.* Wadsworth.

Schuman, Howard and Lawrence Bobo. 1988. "Survey-Based Experiments on White Racial Attitudes toward Residential Integration." *American Journal of Sociology* 94(2): 273–99.

Schumpeter, Joseph. 1950. *Capitalism, Socialism, and Democracy.* New York: Harper & Row.

Smidt, Corwin E. and James M. Penning. 1982. "Religious Commitment, Political Conservatism, and Political and Social Tolerance in the United States: A Longitudinal Analysis." *Sociological Analysis* 43: 231–46.

Sniderman, Paul. 1975. *Personality and Democratic Politics.* Berkeley: University of California Press.

Stark, Rodney. 1997. *The Rise of Christianity: How the Obscure, Marginal Jesus Movement Became the Dominant Religious Force in the Western World in a Few Centuries.* San Francisco: Harper Collins, [1996].

Stark, Rodney. 1999. "Micro Foundations of Religion: A Revised Theory." *Sociological Theory* 17: 264–89.

Stark, Rodney. 2001. *One True God: Historical Consequences of Monotheism*. Princeton: Princeton University Press.

Stark, Rodney. 2003. *For the Glory of God: How Monotheism Led to Reformations, Science, Witch-Hunts, and the End of Slavery.* Princeton: Princeton University Press.

Stark, Rodney. 2005. *The Victory of Reason: How Christianity Led to Freedom, Capitalism, and Western Success.* New York: Random House.

Stark, Rodney and Roger Finke. 2000. *Acts of Faith: Explaining the Human Side of Religion*. Berkeley and Los Angeles: University of California Press.

Steensland, Brian, Jerry Z. Park, Mark D. Regnerus, Lynn D. Robinson, W. Bradford Wilcox, and Robert D. Woodberry. 2000. "The Measure of American Religion: Toward Improving the Sate of the Art." *Social Forces* 79(1): 291–318.

Stetson, Brad and Joseph G. Conti. 2005. *The Truth about Tolerance: Pluralism, Diversity, and the Culture Wars.* Downers Grove, Ill.: InterVarsity.

Stewart, David W., Prem N. Shamdasani, and Dennis W. Rook. 2007. *Focus Groups: Theory and Practice*. 2nd ed. Thousand Oaks, Calif.: Sage.

Stouffer, Samuel. 1992. *Communism, Conformity, and Civil Liberties: A Cross-Section of the Nation Speaks Its Mind*. New Brunswick, N.J.: Transaction Publishers, [1955].

Sullivan, John L., James E. Piereson, and George E. Marcus. 1982. *Political Tolerance and American Democracy.* Chicago: University of Chicago Press.

Sullivan, John L., Pat Walsh, Michal Shamir, David G. Barnum, and James L. Gibson. 1993. "Why Politicians Are More Tolerant: Selective Recruitment and Socialization among Political Elites in Britain, Israel, New Zealand, and the United States." *British Journal of Political Science* 23(1): 51–76.

Wald, Kenneth D. 1997. *Religion and Politics in the United States*. 3rd ed. Washington, D.C.: Congressional Quarterly Press.

Wald, Kenneth D. 2003. *Religion and Politics in the United States*. 4th ed. Lanham, Md.: Rowman & Littlefield.

Wald, Kenneth D., Lyman A. Kellstedt, and David C. Leege. 1993. "Church Involvement and Political Behavior." In *Rediscovering the Religious Factor in American Politics*. Edited by David C. Leege and Lyman A. Kellstedt. Armonk, N.Y.: M. E. Sharpe, 121–38.

Wilcox, Clyde. 1987. "Religious Orientations and Political Attitudes: Variations within the New Christian Right." *American Politics Quarterly* 15(2): 274–96.

Wilcox, Clyde. 2000. *Onward Christian Soldiers? The Religious Right in American Politics.* 2nd ed. Westview Press.

Wilcox, Clyde and Ted G. Jelen. 1990. "Evangelicals and Political Tolerance." *American Politics Quarterly* 18(1): 25–46.

Wilcox, Clyde and Carina Larson. 2006. *Onward Christian Soldiers? The Religious Right in American Politics.* 3rd ed. Westview Press.

Wolfe, Alan. 2003. *The Transformation of American Religion: How We Actually Live Our Faith.* New York: Free Press.

Wood Jr., Robert E. 1979. "Religion and Education: A Continuing Dilemma." *Annals of the American Academy of Political and Social Science* 446: 63–77.

Wuthnow, Robert. 1988. *The Restructuring of American Religion.* Princeton: Princeton University Press.

Index